LEADERSHIP LIVES...

*...in the Infinite Space Between
Management and Skill Set*

MATTHEW J. HESS

authorHOUSE®

AuthorHouse™
1663 Liberty Drive
Bloomington, IN 47403
www.authorhouse.com
Phone: 1 (800) 839-8640

Published by AuthorHouse 09/10/2019

ISBN: 978-1-7283-2655-9 (sc)
ISBN: 978-1-7283-2658-0 (hc)
ISBN: 978-1-7283-2654-2 (e)

TABLE OF CONTEXT

Leadership is abstract, an intangible that
when we see it we know it is present,
and equally, when it leaves, we feel it's absence.

Leaders must react to their followers more than
followers must react to their leader.
That's the nature of leadership. Otherwise, we'd just call it tyranny.

We must know the other person's viewpoint
before we can respond intelligently.

The longer you listen attentively, the more
powerful your words are when you speak.

Intrinsic motivation provides satisfaction that propels
us, feeds our soul and sustains our inner ambition and drive.

Extrinsic Motivation provides fleeting satisfaction
that ultimately leaves us feeling
empty and striving to fill an ever increasing
and insatiable desire for more.

Invest our effort, energy and time at the front-end of the change process
and as change occurs, it will get easier.

As the leader, be the culture we want to create; live it, practice it and tell people about it. We need to fill the Infinite Space between Management and Skill Set with what we want, and what the employee and organization needs.

Improving time management starts with seeing that your own decisions are the reasons we can't seem to manage our own time and schedule.

If a clear goal is not evident, rethink having the meeting.

It doesn't matter how great our content is if no one is listening or interested. We must make ourselves and the content compelling enough to commandeer the audience's attention.

Prejudice is an irrational idea that passes judgment unsubstantiated, and discrimination is acting on that prejudice.

Hire for knowledge, skills and abilities, not other non-job related factors.

A leader should help people grow. Take a caring, compassionate and concerned approach when performing an investigation, corrective action or appraisal.

LEADERSHIP LIVES...IN THE INFINITE SPACE BETWEEN MANAGEMENT AND SKILL SET

PHYSICISTS SEARCHED FOR THE ELUSIVE particle that holds the universe together and gives everything mass since 1964 when Francois Englert and Peter Higgs theorized its existence. In 2012 their theory was proved true. They discovered this particle at CERN, the European Organization for Nuclear Research, using the world's most powerful particle accelerator called the Large Hadron Collider near Geneva, Switzerland.

They called this particle and its field, the Higgs Boson. Its nickname and what most people know it as, is the "God Particle," because it fills the infinite space between all objects in the universe and is responsible for giving objects mass. Without the "God Particle," or if it were to become unstable, what we know and what we see in the universe would break apart and implode.

What does the "God Particle" have to do with leadership? Business scholars and leaders have searched and are still searching for the elusive material that holds business and people together – a silver bullet if you will. There are infinite potentialities in every given situation with every given person, scenario and environment. *Leadership Lives... in the Infinite Space between Management and Skill Set*, just like the "God Particle" fills the infinite space between all objects in the universe. Like the "God Particle," when leadership is unstable and disappears, implosions occur. Scientists theorize that the "God Particle" will remain stable for millions of years, so we have nothing to worry about there, but leadership has proven to be fickle. It comes and goes in an instant without notice. It can be fleeting.

Leadership is arguably even more elusive than the "God Particle." Is leadership even a real thing? The answer is, "Yes," but, how do we prove it? We can't touch it, see it, taste it, or hear it. We only feel it. This is the significant difference between what the "God Particle is and what the idea of Leadership is. The "God Particle" can be observed with our senses while leadership is felt by those around us. The "God Particle" is present all the time, but only detectible for micro moments in time. The good news is we can develop leadership much more cheaply than the 13.25 billion dollars it cost to develop the Large Hadron Collider to locate the "God Particle." Leadership is in all of us, and it's free. When you boil it down to its essence, Leadership is a feeling we give other people. It is not an outcome. We all have the ability to harvest the leadership within us and share it with the world. We simply have to focus, and develop the skills to identify the infinite opportunities for leadership that manifest from moment to moment and fill that space with practical leadership principles.

The "God Particle" unlike leadership is an actual particle, whereas leadership is an intangible, abstract feeling. Just like the "God Particle" fills the Infinite Space between objects and holds the universe together, *Leadership Lives…in the Infinite Space between Management and Skill Set* and holds our businesses and lives together.

The stage on which leadership performs is dynamic, robust and in flux, and then in a moment's notice, the demand for simplicity, generality and stillness are called to center stage and the leader must rewrite the script on the fly.

Leadership includes everything we do or don't do. It's how we interact with people from moment to moment that makes the difference. Management provides parameters and process. Skill sets get work done. Leadership provides direction, inspiration, well-being, greatness and self-actualization.

Thousands of studies have been performed and thousands of books have been written on leadership. Yet still, there is no single pill or ointment to prescribe for leadership. Conversely, there is no single antidote for poor leadership. There is no silver bullet for leadership, period. Organizations often think if we can just make one tweak or make that one critical hire and everything will fall into place. This is no true. If it were that easy, we would just write a prescription and fill leadership voids, every day, all the time.

Instead, we are left with traits, behaviors, models, quotes and anecdotes that express what leadership feels like when it occurs and what the results are when there is a leadership void. We want to understand leadership concepts and apply them appropriately, in real time and at the right time. Every situation is different and requires a different approach. It's not easy, we have to want to understand and continually make adjustments based on the circumstances of each situation.

Leadership is the "God Particle" of life and business. Without leadership the human race devolves and deteriorates into chaos and anarchy just like the universe ceases to exist without the "God Particle."

Life is what happens in the finite space between birth and death, but the pathways and outcomes are infinite when we look at the possibilities and paths that can be taken based on the infinite number of decisions we could make based on the infinite possibilities. Demonstrations of love are what happens in *the Space between* "I love you" in relationships and daily life. Leadership is what happens in *the Space between* hiring an employee and an employee deciding to leave a company or to stay and be satisfied, productive and fulfilled.

Leadership is like water.
It is abstract and takes many forms.
It reacts to its surroundings.
Management is like stone.
It is tangible and takes one form.
Its surroundings react to it.
Like water, leadership changes as soon as you grasp it and drips away.
Like stone, management is easily grasped and stays firm.
Water inspires creativity and innovation to spawn.

Stone refuses to let ideas take root like gravel at the water's edge.
Leadership is the mist that envelopes us.
Management is the cell that contains us.
In fire, water turns to steam, calms the fire
and reconfigures just as strong.
In fire, stone cracks and crumbles from heat and deteriorates into dust.
Water breaks down stone, yet stone can never break down water.

Everything we do as leaders, or say fills *The Infinite Space between Management and Skill Set*. Inspiration, motivation, commitment and greatness are not attained through management and policies they are attained through the intangibles of leadership and what happens in *the Infinite Space between Management and Skill Set*.

Over the course of my life I've observed leaders in sport, business, and life. I have analyzed my own strengths and weakness. The characteristics and traits expressed that result in leadership success vary greatly, situation by situation and person by person. What we give employees and what employees need are often very different. We all have blind spots.

It is common for leaders to have little or no formal leadership training. Leaders in nearly all industries are so heavily focused on skills to perform tasks that we often fail to prepare ourselves to lead and inspire others. This book is intended to identify and provide options to fill *The Infinite Space between Management and Skill Set* with sound leadership acumen, concepts and practices.

Management is easy. Leadership is hard. It is
easy to make rules and enforce them.
It is difficult to inspire people to want to follow them and be great.

Management, rules, regulations, policies and guidelines are essentially the guard rails of an eight lane highway. What happens between those guardrails is leadership. We, as leaders are the drivers and we determine if we crash, stay on course and get to our collective destination on-time and safe.

The possibilities of what will be effective are infinite due to our responses and the dynamics of the environment and situation. This book provides practical, tactical and strategic options for people at all levels to ensure they are using the right tool for every leadership opportunity. We'll look at studies, real-life examples, and proven practices that work if applied at the right time. There isn't a prescription for every situation. That's where our own self-awareness and emotional intelligence guides us. This book will pack your leadership toolbox with the right tool for the occasion. We just need the wisdom to choose the right tool. Sometimes this comes from trial and error and that is ok as long as we assess, learn and hone the art of leadership.

I believe people wake up every morning and want to be great. No one wakes up and says, "Today is going to be terrible and I'm going to wreck everyone's day." No one grows up, gets a job and dreams of failing. It's our job as leaders to help those around us be the best they can be and we do this by understanding that *Leadership Lives... in the Infinite Space between Management and Skill Set.*

CHAPTER 1

THE DIFFERENCES BETWEEN LEADERSHIP AND MANAGEMENT

Overview on Leadership and Management

MANAGEMENT AND LEADERSHIP ARE OFTEN erroneously used synonymously. They are, in fact, nothing alike. Management requires the influencing of tangible things, and leadership requires the influencing of emotion, spirit, motivation and feelings. It is what makes the topic so enigmatic and so difficult to explain from a theoretical perspective. We are left with a bunch of quotes on leadership, and examples of good leadership, but we are not exactly sure how to prescribe leadership. The difference between management and leadership is the difference between the role of a prison warden and the role of a major league baseball manager. Think of it this way;

Processes are managed, people are led.

John Kotter of the Harvard Business School argues that "**Management** is about coping with complexity. Good management brings order and consistency by drawing up formal plans, designing rigid structures and monitoring results against the plans. **Leadership** in contrast, is about coping with change. Leaders establish direction and

1

develop a vision of the future; then they align people by communicating this vision and inspiring them to overcome hurdles."

Like our example of the Prison Warden and MLB Manager, the warden sets rules, and ensures they are obeyed. He is the metaphor for management. He certainly isn't inspiring criminals to greatness, and maybe that's one fundamental flaw with our prison system but, on the other hand, the MLB Manager is the metaphor for leadership. He is not really teaching his players anything, or setting rules of the game, he/she tries to find ways to get the most from the team and inspire a shared vision, mission and goals which ideally culminates in a World Series appearance. The MLB Manager wants his players to be creative and innovative and approach the game of baseball as a team using each of their strengths for the good of the mission, the World Series.

Management *is ensuring a group of people*
adhere to policies and procedures.
Leadership *is the intangible actions of people that inspire greatness.*

The intangibles of leadership inspire us to not only follow policies and procedures but to accomplish our goals in creative and innovative ways. It inspires people to do what some never thought possible; find little nuggets of greatness in themselves and share those with the world, which in turn inspires greatness in others. People then dig into themselves for their own nuggets of greatness to share with the world.

Great leadership inspires great leaders and
that's the essence of leadership.

"In organizing and staffing, **Management** focuses on providing a structure to the work of individuals, their relationships in the organization, and the physical context in which they work. It includes placing people in the right jobs and developing rules and procedures for how the work is to be performed. For **Leadership**, organizing and staffing take the form of communicating a vision to employees, invoking their commitment, and working with them to build teams and coalitions useful in fulfilling the organization's mission." (Northouse, 8-9)

*Leadership is like water. It is abstract in that it takes many forms
and reacts to its surroundings. Management is like stone. It is
tangible and takes one form. Its surroundings react to it.
Like water, leadership changes as soon as you grasp it and drips away.
Like stone, management is easily grasped and stays firm.
Water inspires creativity and innovation to spawn.
Stone refuses to let ideas take root like gravel at the water's edge.
Leadership is the mist that envelopes us.
Management is the cell that contains us.
In fire, water turns to steam, calms the fire
and comes back again just as strong.
In fire, stone cracks and crumbles from heat and deteriorates into dust.
The collective power of water breaks down stone,
yet stone can never break down water.*

The reason it is so difficult to theorize leadership or give a step-by-step explanation as to how to be a leader is because, as we may imagine, leadership is something that happens all the time and varies with each decision on a moment to moment basis. It is fluid like water. It is organic and complex and requires constant reevaluation. To explain how someone illustrated good leadership would mean being able to decode the workings of their brain. Instead, what we are left with are characteristics of leaders, examples of leaders and a few models as to what characteristics and traits leaders have and how they fall within a given style of leadership.

*Management is easy. Leadership is hard.
It is easy to make rules and enforce them.
It is difficult to get people to want to follow them.*

Leadership Styles

Charismatic Leadership – (John F. Kennedy, Martin Luther King Jr., Steve Jobs, Mary Kay Ash, Ted Turner, and Bill Clinton)

Charismatic Leadership Theory states that followers make attributions of heroic or extraordinary leadership abilities when they observe certain behaviors. Five characteristics of the charismatic leader have been isolated:

1. **Vision and Articulation**: Has a vision – expressed as an idealized goal – that proposes a future better than the status quo and is able to clarify the importance of the vision in terms that are understandable to others.
2. **Personal Risk**: Willing to take on high personal risk, incur high costs and engage in self-sacrifice to achieve the vision.
3. **Environmental Sensitivity**: Able to make realistic assessments of the environmental constraints and resources needed to bring about change.
4. **Sensitivity to Follower Needs**: Perceptive of others' abilities and responsive to their needs and feelings.
5. **Unconventional Behavior:** Engages in behaviors that are perceived as novel and counter to norms. (Robbins, 343)

Transactional Leaders – are managers who guide their people through established goals and parameters by clarifying role and task requirements. This style falls under the definition of management.

Transformational Leaders – are leaders who inspire followers to transcend their own self-interests and are capable of having a profound and extraordinary effect on followers.

Transformational leadership is built on top of Transactional Leadership and the two should not be viewed as opposing ways of getting things done but, generally, we do not get to transformation, without transaction.

In other words, if we view these latter two types of leadership and separate their essence, we notice that Transactional Leadership is more like Management and Transformational Leadership is more in line with our definitions of Leadership. Again, we often use the two words synonymously when, the fact remains, we can call it whatever we want, but there are significant differences between managers and leaders.

Managers aren't necessarily leaders,
and leaders aren't always managers.
It is the ability to get things done and make people feel good
about what they've done that makes a leader a leader.
Managers hide behind policy and leaders
create inspiration toward greatness.

Evidence supports the superiority of transformational leadership over transactional leadership (management) with impressive consistency. For example, a number of studies with US, Canadian, and German military officers found, at every level, that transformational leaders were evaluated as more effective than their transactional counterparts. And Managers at FedEX who were rated by their followers as exhibiting more transformational leadership were evaluated by their immediate supervisors as higher performers and more promotable. In summary, the overall evidence indicates that transformational leadership is more strongly correlated than transactional leadership with lower turnover rates, higher productivity and higher employee satisfaction. (Robbins, 344)

Characteristics of Transactional and Transformational Leaders

Transactional Leader – (Management)

- Contingent Reward – Contracts the exchange of rewards for effort, promises rewards for good performance, and may recognize accomplishments.
- Management by Exception – (Active) – Watches and searches for deviations from rules and standards and takes corrective action.
- Management by Exception – (Passive) – Intervenes only if standards are not met.
- Laissez Faire – Abdicates responsibilities, and avoids making decisions.

Transformational Leader – (Leadership)

- Charisma – Provides vision and a sense of mission, instills pride, gains respect and trust.
- Inspiration – Communicates high expectations, uses symbols to focus efforts, expresses important purposes in simple ways.
- Intellectual Stimulation – Promotes intelligence, rationality and careful problem solving.
- Individualized Consideration – Gives personal attention, treats each employee individually, coaches and advises. (Robbins, 344)

Visionary Leadership - (Examples, - Michael Dell, Rupert Murdoch, Mary Kay Ash)

Visionary Leadership is the ability to create and articulate a realistic, credible, attractive vision of the future for an organization or organizational unit that grows out of and improves upon the present. This vision, if properly selected and implemented is so energizing that it in effect jump-starts the future by calling forth the skills, talents and resources to make it happen.

Generally, there have been three leadership traits that visionary leader's exhibit.

1. **Excellent Communicator** – the ability to explain the vision to others.
2. **Integrity** – Express the vision not only through words, but behavior.
3. **Extend the vision to different contexts** – the ability to make marketing, accounting and every other area see their relevance and how they fit. (Robbins, 344)

Emotional Intelligence and Leadership Effectiveness

Intelligence or IQ is important to success, but in effect IQ is simply an example of minimum requirements or skills for the job. It is usually demonstrated through the attainment of degrees or certifications as a baseline for minimum requirements. IQ and technical skills are necessary, but they do not predict who will rise up to be the leader. The best indicator to predict who will emerge as an informal or formal leader is the person with the highest Emotional Quotient or EQ. Possessing and demonstrating the five components of EQ are essential requirements for leadership success.

EQ Components for Leadership

1. **Self- awareness** – Exhibited by self-confidence, realistic self-assessment, and self-deprecating humor.
2. **Self-management** – Exhibited by trustworthiness and integrity, comfort with ambiguity, and openness to change.
3. **Self-motivation** – Exhibited by a strong drive to achieve, optimism and high organizational commitment.
4. **Empathy** – Exhibited by expertise in building and retaining talent, cross-cultural sensitivity and service to clients and customers.
5. **Social Skills** – Exhibited by the ability to lead change, persuasiveness and expertise in building and leading teams. (Robbins, 346.)

Leadership isn't about how smart we are, how skilled we are or how high our grades are, it's about understanding what it means to be an emotional human being and then tap into that commonality to inspire others to find greatness within themselves.

Inspiration and Leadership Can Occur Everywhere

I am an ordained minister. I was ordained in five minutes through the Universal Life Church – on-line. I became ordained so I could officiate the ceremony of a buddy of mine from college – the same guy that you'll learn later flew across the country to WVU to bombard the Dean to be accepted to Grad School.

Since then, I've performed 7 weddings. Anyway, I performed the ceremony for the nephew of a buddy of mine whose wedding I actually performed as well. The wedding was thrown together. At the rehearsal dinner, there was no plan. They told me they were writing their vows via email prior to that day. They didn't. We stood at the podium; the bride, groom, two groomsmen and three bridesmaids. They looked at me to start the ceremony. I looked around and said, "We're lopsided up here." The groom said, "Chad shot up yesterday. He's out."

I didn't ask questions, but noticed that the best man was horrified and embarrassed at the same time. I asked for the vows. Panic covered the bride and groom's faces. They didn't do it. I told them I would put together a ceremony that evening and everything would be fine. The next day the wedding went off without a hitch. People cried. We walked out of the "chapel" and into the "reception hall." The best man stood to give his speech. He was nervous, and unsure of himself. His voice quivered. He powered through and gave what I thought to be an amazing, sincere, and inspiring speech, especially given the circumstances.

Later that evening around a bonfire at the "after party", I slid in next to him, held out my hand, and said, "You gave an excellent speech." He smiled and said, "Thanks. I wanted it to be good because Tyler and his mom were a huge part of my life. They provided a lot of stability for me." We talked and he divulged to me that he had been trying to get into grad schools, but had been rejected so many times he couldn't put a number on it.

I told him a story about a friend of mine that I lived with in California after we graduated from Ohio University. I told him the only way my buddy was accepted into Grad school was because he got on a plane and went to WVU and walked into the Dean's office to plead his case directly and in person.

*I kicked the best man in the proverbial *ss every time he came up with a reason why he wasn't going to get into grad school. We talked for over an hour. I gave him my business card and told him to call me if he needed anything, and to tell me when he got accepted somewhere. The email below is what he sent me many months later. It made my day. The leadership he demonstrated by doing this, is what will make him tremendously satisfied and successful.*

Hey Matt,

We met several months ago at Tyler Weltzer's wedding. I was the best man and you had some motivational words for me as we talked at Gayla's after the wedding. At the time, it was exactly the kick in the *ss I needed to stay motivated after getting rejection after rejection. I've attached a picture of the wall next to my computer at home. I stuck your card up there with a little motivational poster when I need to remind myself to stay focused.

You wanted me to shoot you an e-mail once I made some progress, so I just wanted to write and let you know I was accepted into the Fisheries and Mari culture graduate program at Texas A&M - Corpus Christi. I'll be starting in the fall. I'm eager to be out of Ohio and moving onto bigger and better things. Thanks for saying the things I needed to hear at the time. It definitely played a big role in my getting accepted.

All the best,
Ethan Taulbe

Photo below

Just for clarity sake, Ethan was 22 and after I wrote back and told him how he made my day and how the poster was absolutely perfect, especially for the world we live in with all of its noise and distractions, he sent me a photo of the poster above.

Consider Ethan's story as you watch the upcoming video from Drew Dudley on Everyday Leadership and who has had an impact on your life. Did you tell them about it?

Leadership Theories

There are many different theories on leadership. **Trait Theories,** which try to focus on the traits of leaders and then correlate those traits to successful leadership were popular early on and are finding resurgence in the last twenty years. The problem with Trait Theory was that traits were not universally attributed to effective leaders. Some had these traits and others didn't, yet leadership success still occurred.

This spawned the idea that **Behavior Theories** may shed more light on the matter of identifying and predicting leadership if researchers could identify leadership behaviors. The implications of this would mean that leaders could be taught to use certain behaviors and therefore could be trained to be leaders. Leadership would be abundant and leaders could be made. However, if Trait Theory proved true, then leaders were born, not made. To the dismay of Behavior Theorists their theories proved somewhat unreliable and had moderate success at best. The question as to whether or not leaders are born or are made is still under debate. It's the old discussion of nature or nurture. There is probably some validity in both ideas, but pinpointing anything has proven elusive to researchers in identifying the tangibles of leadership, putting them in a box and selling them as a product.

*Leadership is an abstract and an intangible that
when you see it you know it is present,
and equally, when it leaves, you feel it's absence.*

What researchers discovered was that situations and environmental factors were critical to the success or failure of a leader in any given situation. This invoked the idea of **Contingency Theories**. It is the idea that a leader has to be in the right place at the right time with the right skills, abilities, knowledge, and traits to find success. For example, if Martin Luther King Jr. were born in the early1800's, would he have been a civil rights leader even if everything else were the same? The answer is most likely, "no." The environment wasn't conducive to that type of change. Timing, skill, and readiness of those willing to be lead have to be aligned as well. MLK Jr. would likely have still been a powerful leader, but it would have likely been in another arena.

The stage on which leadership performs is dynamic, robust
and in flux, and then in a moment's notice, the demand
for simplicity, generality and stillness are called to center
stage and the leader must rewrite the script on the fly.

Leaders understand that no prescribed way is always the right way. Circumstances outside of our control often dictate which set of skills or which leadership style may function most effectively. Great leaders strive to adapt their style and approach based on circumstances.

It is like the fluidity of water, not the rigidness
of stone that a leader adapts, bends,
flows and gets creative to overcome the next obstacle.

Drew Dudley, the Former Leadership Development Coordinator at the University of Toronto, and current CEO of Nuance Leadership Development Services believes that leadership is within us all every day and that we just need to change the way we define leadership.

"Leadership is not a characteristic reserved for
the extraordinary." (Drew Dudley)

He believes that leadership is something we are all capable of but that we have attributed extraordinary abilities to those who exhibit leadership of incredible proportions, thereby putting "leadership" out of our grasps.

"You have made someone's life better by something you said or did. If you think you haven't you are just one of the people that haven't been told. It's scary to think of ourselves as that powerful, it can be frightening that we can matter that much to people, as long as we keep leadership bigger than us, something beyond us, as long as we make it about changing the world, we give ourselves an excuse not to expect it every day, from ourselves and each other." (Drew Dudley)

Drew Dudley – *"Everyday Leadership"*
http://www.ted.com/talks/lang/en/drew_dudley_everyday_leadership. html

Tell the person that made your life better how they affected you. The act of sharing that information is leadership.

Everyday Leadership

I was fortunate in a sense to have had three fathers. I wish I didn't need three, but that's the way things worked out. I'm still not sure if I'm a very good dad, but at least I have three different people to pull from. One was my biological father. Another was my step-father. The third was my best friend's dad. If I could have merged my two dads I would have had one solid Dad.

My bio-dad provided half the puzzle to fatherhood – he made me feel smart, strong and he listened to me. He focused on leadership. He didn't pay child support and let me do whatever I wanted when my brother and I visited him in Florida. He, in a sense, provided emotional support from 1000 miles away, at his convenience.

My step-father provided none of these attributes. He was emotionally vacant and even seemed to resent me, but he was very generous and used "things," and financial support as a control mechanism as a substitute for caring.

My best friend's dad, was what I most aspired to be like. He would correct me when I was out of line without belittling me. When I came home from college, I would sometimes not go to my house, but would stay with my best friend and his family. My friend's father would hug me, and hand me ten bucks and say, "Boy, get you some gas for the drive back." He took us to the high school basketball games, and played with us in the street when we were kids. We sat on the front porch with him and his brother for hours and listened, and laughed at their stories and commentaries on life. It wasn't until later in my life, when I was in my thirties, that what I'm explaining crystalized into a coherent understanding of what was actually going on amongst my "three" dads.

When this came into focus, after I'd had two boys of my own, I went over to his house one afternoon and told him. I said, "Mike, if it weren't for you, I don't know where I'd be right now. You always looked out for me. You showed me what a good father is. I love you." It was as if he was waiting to hear those words his entire life. He teared up a little bit, grabbed me by the back of the head and brought me in for a hug. He said, "I love you too, boy."

Don't get me wrong, he was also the guy that would yell at my friend and I when we came in and gulped down the milk his mother had on the table for dinner and say, "G*d d*mnit, boys! Milk's not for quenchin' your thirst. Drink some water." My friend's mother would say, "Hess, you can drink whatever you want." I'd glance at my third dad. He'd squint at me and show his teeth like he was growling. The point is that when someone does something for you, extends kindness, and shows you the way, let them know it. Expressing that appreciation is leadership.

Leadership Types

To understand the various types of leaders and the way they view the world, it is important to understand the situations in which these styles can be most effective. These are very broad and cannot be laid over a group of people, situation or environment like a blanket and expect everyone to be warm and fuzzy. They are guidelines.

Autocratic Leaders – make all decisions and then tell employees what must be done and how to do it. An autocratic style of leadership is generally needed to stimulate unskilled, unmotivated people. It is a good approach when circumstances require a quick decision and time is of the essence. In modern management practice it is not a favorable approach. Think small doses.

Democratic Leaders – involve their employees in decisions. The leader presents a situation and encourages subordinates to express opinions and contribute ideas. Highly skilled, trained and motivated people generally respond better to democratic leadership.

Free-Rein Leaders – let their employees work without much interference. The managers set performance standards and allow employees to find their own ways to meet them. For this style to be effective, employees must know what the standards are, and they must be motivated to attain the standards. The free-rein style of leadership can be a powerful motivator because it demonstrates a great deal of trust and confidence in the person. Highly skilled, trained and motivated employees may respond better to this style. Democratic and free-rein are leadership styles that reflect the change in the workforce from labor to knowledge workers and will be discussed further in the Diversity and the Changing Management Paradigm Chapter.

Contingency Leadership

*Let's imagine you are a **Free-Rein** leader and your team is highly effective. They value their autonomy and are glad to use you as a resource for problems they struggle with. Then one day a group comes to you and after speaking with them, you realize that they have taken serious short cuts in patient care. They have missed the valuable point that specific documentation must occur for the doctor and other care providers to be on the same page. Because of this misguided efficiency tactic the staff has taken, a patient has been given a double dose of high level pain medication and intervention is required.*

*As a **Free-Rein** leader, your natural instinct is to tell them to fix it and report back once it is handled. Would this be effective leadership? Probably not. There is a crisis. You gave them autonomy and they took it to a place that has caused harm to a patient albeit unintentional, yet they overlooked some basic measures of safety and failed to understand the point* *of doing it correctly. Their priorities became misaligned with the goals of the organization which were to provide excellent patient care. As the leader, we should engage the problem, understand it, and correct it immediately. There wasn't time to talk about it, it needed corrected immediately.*

Step one: mitigate any further problems and Step two: illustrate the importance of not repeating "efficiency shortcuts." The leader should intervene and immediately take corrective action to right the course of the ship which is to realign the goals of the organization with the work of the staff. This is done through **Autocratic Leadership** *– tell people what to do and how to do it. People should not be demeaned or made to feel as if they were malicious or stupid but the issue needs to be discussed. It isn't a finger pointing session; it is an opportunity for the leader to demonstrate quality leadership.*

Once we've corrected the issue, and asked staff how they arrived at that patient care decision, we determine where they veered from the mission, why they veered and then explain why the correct path was different. Invoke the **Democratic Leadership Style** *because our spur of the moment decision may not have been the best decision, but it was necessary at the time to stop the situation from drifting further off course. Ask the staff if they have any better ideas than what you came up with and make sure to align the suggested goals with organizational goals. Remember, if people have say in a decision, they will buy-in to it and own it.*

*Just like a carpenter or nurse uses different sized
nails and needles for different situations,
a leader uses different approaches dependent on the situation at hand.*

Leadership Characteristics

After all the research, and all the top ten lists of leadership qualities, traits and characteristics, there still seems to be no firm and agreed upon absolute. With that said, there certainly is no prescribed step-by-step process that will ensure we become an effective leader. However, there was a book written by the Chairman and CEO of Tom Peters Group/Learning Systems, James Kouzes and the Dean of the Leavey School of Business and Administration at Santa Clara University, Barry

Posner, called *The Leadership Challenge*. In this award winning and influential book, they identified through analyzing thousands of cases and surveys, ten common and fundamental leadership commitments. The key is to understand these and put them to practice at the right time and in the right situation. We must be honest with ourselves. Do we practice these commitments?

Ten Fundamental Leadership Commitments – Kouzes and Posner – *The Leadership Challenge*

A. Challenging the Process

1. *Search for opportunities* - to change the status quo. Look for innovative ways to improve the organization.
2. *Experiment and take risks* - since risk taking involves mistakes and failure, leaders accept the inevitable disappointments as learning opportunities.

B. Inspire a shared vision

3. *Envision an uplifting and ennobling future*
4. *Enlist others in a common vision* - by appealing to their values, interests, hopes and dreams.

C. Enabling Others to Act

5. *Foster collaboration* - by promoting cooperative goals and building trust.
6. *Strengthen people* - by giving power away, providing choice, and developing competence, assigning critical tasks, and offering visible support.

D. Modeling the Way

7. *Set the example* - by behaving in ways that are consistent with shared values.

8. *Achieve small wins* - that promote consistent progress and build commitment.

E. Encouraging the Heart

9. *Recognize individual contributions* - to the success of every project.
10. *Celebrate team accomplishments* - regularly. (Kousez and Posner, 18)

Characteristics Constituents Admire in Leaders

This study by Kouzes and Posner asked thousands of people from four continents, (mostly from the US), to "Select the seven qualities that they most look for and admire in a leader, someone whose direction they would willingly follow." The results were...

Characteristics	% Choosing	Characteristics	% Choosing
Honest	88	Courageous	29
Forward Looking	75	Cooperative	28
Inspiring	68	Imaginative	28
Competent	63	Caring	23
Fair-Minded	49	Determined	17
Supportive	41	Mature	13
Broad Minded	40	Ambitious	13
Intelligent	40	Loyal	11
Straightforward	33	Self-Controlled	5
Dependable	32	Independent	5

As you will notice from the above list, the characteristics that people, who are being asked to follow leaders look for are generally in-line with the Ten Fundamental Leadership Commitments. However, they are not exactly in-line. There is always variation between the lists of traits, qualities and characteristics successful leaders possess, but that is academia for you. This of course lends itself to the enigmatic, intangible and abstract myths surrounding leadership. What we believe to be good leadership skills may be in some situations, but not in others. What leaders feel to be strong and just qualities in themselves may not be viewed similarly in the eyes of their followers. It is critical for leaders to be tuned-in, have their finger on the pulse of their constituents and constantly feel around for clues as to the collective mind set of the group and the individuals.

There will also be **informal leaders** that influence group dynamics and those people are key players in the formal and informal attitudes of the group. A good leader knows who those people are and searches for ways to enlist them into the value system, goal orientation and structure of the group to not only the group's benefit, but the leader's benefit as well. Remember, the group and the leader live and die together.

*Leadership is to understand the needs of the people
we try to influence and then give them what they need
and still accomplish organizational goals.*

Clearly from Kouzes and Posner's list above, there are many leadership traits valued by those asked to follow. These various traits or "needs" rear their heads in various situations. **Emotional Intelligence,** or the ability to engage and have meaningful relationships with others, again, comes pouring back to the forefront of the leadership discussion.

*It is through Emotional Intelligence that leaders adapt, understand,
empathize and react to the changing needs of their constituents.
People are from different backgrounds; socio-economic, education,
familial, race, gender and religious. With these differences, people
have varying values, ideas of justice, and needs. We, as leaders need
to be tuned in to perceive their needs (or we can ask what they are)
and provide the direction **they** need, not what **we** think they need.*

Famous Leadership Quotes as Related to Kousez and Posner's Ten Fundamental Leadership Commitments

Let's look now at how influential people over the millennia have viewed leadership and see how their ideas fit into the modern-day Ten Fundamental Leadership Commitments of Kouzes and Posner.

Leadership means seeing and understanding that things can be bigger than ourselves.

Challenge the Process

1. Search for Change Opportunities

Harry S. Truman – US President – 1945-1953
"Men make history and not the other way around. In periods where there is no leadership, society stands still. Progress occurs when courageous, skillful leaders seize the opportunity to change things for the better."

Susan Jeffers – Ph.D. 1938-2012
"Knowing that we can make a difference in this world is a great motivator. How can we know this and not be involved?"

2. Experiment and Take Risks

Russell H. Ewing – Iconic Chicago Broadcaster
"A boss creates fear, a leader confidence. A boss fixes blame, a leader corrects mistakes. A boss knows all, a leader asks questions. A boss makes work drudgery, a leader makes it interesting. A boss is interested in himself or herself, a leader is interested in the group."

George Patton – 1912 Olympian (Pentathlon) and Lieutenant General US Military

"Don't tell people how to do things, tell them what to do and let them surprise you with their results."

Inspire a Shared Vision

3. Envision the Future

Woodrow Wilson – US President – 1913-1921
"Absolute identity with one's cause is the first and great condition of successful leadership."

Theodore M. Hesburgh – President of The University of Notre Dame 1952-1987
"The very essence of leadership is that you must have vision. You can't blow an uncertain trumpet."

Proverbs 29:18 – God – known as the creator of all things
"Where there is no vision, the people perish."

4. Enlist Others in a Common Vision

Lao Tzu – 5th-4th Century BC Chinese Philosopher, known as founder of Taoism
"Go to the people. Learn from them. Live with them. Start with what they know. Build with what they have. The best of leaders, when the job is done, when the task is accomplished, the people will say we have done it ourselves."
Nelson Mandela – South African President and Anti-Apartheid Activist
"It is better to lead from behind and to put others in front, especially when you celebrate victory when nice things occur. You take the front-line when there is danger. Then people will appreciate your leadership."

Enable Others to Act

5. Foster Collaboration

**Mahatma Gandhi (Great Soul) – Led
India to Independence through
Non-Violent Civil Disobedience**
*"I suppose leadership at one time meant muscles; but
today it means getting along with people."*

Dwight D. Eisenhower – US President 1953-1961
*"Leadership is the art of getting someone else to do
something you want done because he wants to do it."*

**Henry Gilmer – Former Mayor of Cambridge,
Massachusetts – 1832-1891**
*"Look over your shoulder now and then to
be sure someone's following you."*

6. Strengthen People

John Quincy Adams – US President 1825-1829
*"If your actions inspire others to dream more, learn more,
do more and become more, you are a leader."*

Jim Rohn – Author, Entrepreneur 1930-2009
*"A good objective of leadership is to help those who are doing poorly
to do well and to help those who are doing well to do even better."*

Dwight D. Eisenhower - US President 1953-1961
*"You don't lead by hitting people over the
head - that's assault, not leadership."*

John D. Rockefeller – Oil Industrialist & Philanthropist 1839-1937
*"Good leadership consists of showing average people
how to do the work of superior people."*

Rosalynn Carter – First Lady of the US 1977-1981
*"A leader takes people where they want to go. A great leader takes
people where they don't necessarily want to go, but ought to be."*

Model the Way

7. **Set the Example**

Barack Obama – US President 2008-present
*"We can't drive our SUVs and eat as much as we want
and keep our homes on 72 degrees at all times... and then
just expect that other countries are going to say OK.
That's not leadership. That's not going to happen."*

**Albert Schweitzer – Theologian, Organist, Philosopher,
Physician, Medical Missionary 1875-1965**
"Example is leadership."

Robert Half – Founder of Robert Half International, S&P 500
"Delegating work, works, provided the one delegating works, too."

8. **Achieve Small Wins**

Patrick Lencioni – Author and Business Consultant
*"As a leader, you're probably not doing a good job unless your
employees can do a good impression of you when you're not around."*

Margaret Mead – Cultural Anthropologist 1901-1978
*"Never doubt that a small group of thoughtful
committed citizens can change the world.
Indeed, it is the only thing that ever has."*

Carly Fiorina, CEO Hewlett Packard 1999-2005
"Leadership comes in small acts as well as bold strokes."

Encourage the Heart

9. Recognize Individuals

Max DuPree - CEO Herman Miller Furniture/Author
*"The first responsibility of a leader is to define
reality. The last is to say thank you.
In between, the leader is a servant."*

Rosabeth Moss Kantor – Tenured Harvard Business Professor
*"Leaders are more powerful role models when
they learn than when they teach."*

Arnold H. Glasgow
*"A good leader takes a little more than his share of the blame,
and a little less than his share of the credit."*

10. Celebrate

Robert Burton – 1577-1640 English Scholar
"I light my candle from their torches."

Ovid (Publius Ovidius Naso) Roman Poet 43BC – 17AD
"A ruler should be slow to punish and swift to reward."

In Summary

These quotes cover a large span of time and culture. After reviewing them, one thing is abundantly clear, leadership is a concept, like love, that people feel universally. Like love, we can only speak about it in metaphor, analogy, narrative, and what it isn't. Like love, leadership is felt and exhibited through sincerity, honesty, integrity, compassion, visions of the future and collaboration with others when one realizes that things may just be larger than ourselves. Leadership and Love aren't something we can touch, see, or taste, but we know when it arrives and we know when it leaves. The only way to illustrate either effectively is to demonstrate their intangible qualities through our actions and simply do it!

We fill *the Infinite Space between Management and Skill Set,* with real leadership action. Just like we fill *the Space between* "I love you's" to our spouses/significant others with our actions to prove our love, we must do the same with leadership. Saying you're in love and acting in love and saying you're a leader and acting like a leader are two different things. Fill *the Infinite Space between Management and Skill Set* with actions that make people either feel love, or feel leadership.

Try! And if we fail, we learn from it. If we learn, we are successful and we've taken the first and most important step toward becoming a better leader.

CHAPTER 2

DIVERSITY AND THE CHANGING MANAGEMENT PARADIGM

A Brief History

A CHANGING WORK ENVIRONMENT IS inevitable. Often the greatest factor affecting this is the actual workforce and how they view work. The largest variable that leaders face in a changing business climate is how we adapt to changing generational perspectives. First, is a leader able to see and understand the changes in the environment and are we able to see the changes in people as simply different, rather than inferior or superior? Second, can a leader apply what we've learned and adapt to changes? Too often leaders try to cram their perspective down the throats of the people they are asking to follow them, when in reality it is the leader's responsibility to treat each person as an individual and lead them the way "they" want, and need to be led.

If you force feed people sh*t sandwiches, they will vomit all over you.

To see differences in people objectively, we have to understand what has caused these changes. There are barriers between each generation. Each builds their viewpoint based on different experiences in time. To be 18 years old in 1991 is considerably different than being 18 years old in 2016. Because generational experiences are so different, it is common for each new generation to view the up and coming generation negatively without considering that different isn't always worse, it is just different. Below were common criticisms of Baby Boomers regarding Gen X'ers.

I don't know what's wrong with this generation, whatever you call it,
Gen X, Gen X games, whatever. Their work
ethic is terrible and they don't care.
They're job hoppers and they're only concerned with themselves.

It even goes back to the WWII generation, (The Traditional Generation) that gave birth to the Baby Boomers.

They're out of control, radicals, all they want to do is
drugs and have sex with anything that moves. Where's
the modesty? You can't get them to do any work.
My gosh they stink, and that hair.

Now, even today, we still hear similar sentiments echoed by Generation X, about Generation Y.

Generation Y, why is the question, why are they so lazy, and why
aren't they loyal? Why don't they care about anything? Why can't
they work as hard as me? They don't want to do anything except
play video games and text message, why? Why do they feel so
entitled? It's ridiculous. #we'reallbeautifulindividualsnowflakes

It's not exactly clear at this point what Millennials will say about the i Gen (Gen Z) which is the latest group entering the workforce, but we'll take a stab at it. Depending on which classification of years we use to define them, 1995-2012, some could be 23 years old now. I imagine, though, Millennials will say something like;

i Gen, or Gen Z – pick one, it's just like their gender – can't decide –
am I an individual or a Zombie? I don't know?! Of course it's the "I" Gen,
all they think about is themselves. They don't listen to anyone. They're

afraid of life because it's actually happening in reality. It's as if no one knows anything unless it's presented in a video shorter than a minute.

It's as if each generation can't stop to remember how they were viewed and how they were treated, because with each new generation the same treatment they didn't like is passed on to the up and coming generation. The key to remember is that the new generation is responding to the old generation and, most often, the things they didn't like about it. As Jack White of the White Stripes says, "You can't take the effect and make it the cause."

There is a theme from generation to generation. It is that the generation in power is right and the generation who wants power is wrong and therefore must be subjugated for the continued power of the older generation. It's a perpetual cycle that can only be broken through understanding and adaptability. Remember, one size does not fit all. We cannot throw a blanket over a group of people and expect them to all be comfortable.

Diversity is the spark of innovation and creativity.

There are very clear reasons as to why these generations see the world of work differently; self-esteem, involvement, teams, empowerment and most importantly, a desire to balance work-life with family and personal lives. The need for employees to look out for their own best interests and feel satisfied in their work life has become paramount in the business world. Generation X threw the ally-oop and Generation Y is taking this idea and slamming it home. We can all learn from one other. We don't have to necessarily understand, but we do need to accept.

The Changing Social Contract

*"The **social contract** of the past was an implicit understanding between employers and employees that hard work and loyalty would result in continued employment. This was prevalent in prior years. However, it does seem to be true that for a growing number of organizations, they cannot maintain this contract. The assumption that hard work*

and loyalty from employees will be matched by the job security
provided by the employer is no longer as valid as it once was."
- (French, 51)

Why the Social Contract Has Changed

Globalization or the breaking down of trade barriers between countries started social contract changes. It became easier to do business in other countries. Because of globalization, **outsourcing** or moving operations to foreign nations increased and many companies took their manufacturing out of the U.S. due to lower wages and fewer regulations. This left the U.S. economy stagnant and with a loss of good, strong, blue-collar jobs. The manufacturing sector was outsourced. As a result, labor jobs moved to places like China and an increase for technology, construction and service workers occurred in the U.S. as the aging Baby Boomer population retires.

The problem for many years was that the educational level of the U.S. wasn't at the level needed to perform the knowledge jobs that slowly replaced labor jobs. The shift from **labor jobs to knowledge jobs** occurred quicker than the U.S. could react due to mass outsourcing internationally. Unemployment lent itself to the reeducation of the U.S. Finally, with an increasingly educated nation, often in service oriented jobs such as nursing and healthcare, the expectations of what work meant, changed. Construction and manufacturing jobs dried up during the recession, and in their place, service and IT jobs came to the forefront which spawned vocational colleges and for-profit education that quickly filled the gap. Now, there is a deficit in blue collar workers needed to develop infrastructure and keep the U.S. growing to meet the demand of population expansion because Gen X was coerced to college and to abandon trades.

Generational leadership changes are constantly happening as well; out with the old and in with the new. It is a constant cycle that perplexes each new generation as they fight for influence and control over their work life. Currently, there is a shift as Baby Boomers exit the workforce and Generation X replaces them in management roles. With this, Generation Y is stepping into the roles that Generation X is vacating and they're bringing their own flavor, ideas and definition of what work means to them.

However, all of this stair stepping was stagnated in the mid -2000's due to poor stock market performance, the real estate market crashing and retirements being postponed during the recession. Baby-Boomers are staying in the workforce longer than they had planned which has caused Generation X to stay lower on the workforce totem for longer than they planned which ultimately doesn't as many new positions for Generation Y. Because of this and many other reasons we'll discover later, the various generations view their worlds of work very differently.

Generational Characteristics

"1946-1964"	"1965-1979"	"1980-1994"	1995-2012
80 Million	44-50 Million	70 Million	69 Million
Baby Boomers	**Generation X**	**Generation Y**	**iGen/Gen Z**
Fair day's work	Accountability,	Tech Savvy,	Tolerant of Cultures,
for a fair day's pay.	Teamwork,	Family Centric,	Sexual Orientation, Races
Loyal, Hard Working,	Innovation,	Confident/Ambitious,	Cautious, risk avoidance
Security, Low Risk	Participation,	Achievement Oriented,	Less likely to go to church
Don't Question Authority	Empowerment,	Crave Feedback,	Think for themselves -
	Question Authority	Team Oriented	government and church not seen as authorities

The Reasons for Generational Differences

There are the inevitable changes that occur as cultures and societies develop, such as increased efficiency and evolution of thought. The evolution is generally toward a kinder, more gentle and inclusive way of seeing the world and its inhabitants. If one was to characterize the differences between the Traditional Generation, the Baby Boomers, Generation X, Generation Y and the iGen or Gen Z it would be summarized as more equalitarian way of viewing the world of management, work and family. You will often hear the prior generation talk about how tough they had it, but remember, the generation before them talked about how much softer they were than them, just like they do with the new generation. Listen carefully to yourself, because you'll likely do the same thing to the generation that comes after you. How has this happened and why?

Socialization, living arrangements, economy, work, technology, consumerism, family and cultural diversity are the aspects of this change we need to look at to understand the differences. Second, we will try to understand how to adapt and assimilate all generations into a cohesive work unit.

Leaders must react to their followers more than
the followers must react to their leader.
That's the nature of leadership. Otherwise, we'd just call it tyranny.

The key is to understand what made these generational groups different and how those differences affect the way they see the world, and work.

Simon Sinek details some of the reasons Millennials appear different and interact differently than any other generation in the past.

"Most Leaders Don't Even Know the Game they are in," Live to Lead 2016 – Simon Sinek
https://youtu.be/RyTQ5-SQYTo

Socialization in short is to fit into or train for a social environment, to adapt to social needs, or to participate actively in a social group. Each generation grows up in very different political, economic, and social environments, and because these groups have learned and adapted in different ways to their environment, surroundings and socio-economic pressures, they can't help but be different.

A society that lives on the river, will be good swimmers and fishermen,
while another society that lives in the plains will be good
hunters and farmers. The environments in which socialization
occurred are different so they learn and adapt differently.
Don't judge, learn from the differences and embrace them.

The statistics below illustrate to us why one group seeks independence and the other group is dependent, and why one group may value family and the other may value work, but most importantly look at how the environments of these groups in their youth, transformed their ideas on authority and other aspects of work.

Generational Differences

Socialization

Baby Boomers

- First TV sets
- Were cared for by their mothers mostly – and at home.

Generation X

- Spent 12,000 lifetime hours in front of a teacher and 20,000 lifetime hours in front of a TV.
- Were socialized by the TV and in some cases it taught them to tie their shoes, count, and spell while both parents worked - Sesame Street!
- The first generation to have no legal segregation in their lifetime.

Generation Y - Millennials

- Nurtured and pampered by parents, socialized by computers, and technology is part of life.
- Is of the "No Person Left Behind" Generation.

iGen or Gen Z

- First generation to spend their entire childhood on a smart phone.

- Less likely to drive, work, drink alcohol, date, have sex, or go out of the house without their parents.

Living Arrangements

Baby Boomers

- Own homes, and live alone mostly, (except for their Generation X'er children who couldn't leave the house, or keep landing there periodically through their lives.)

Generation X

- X'ers couldn't leave home and it's not because they didn't have ideas of personal freedom and independence it was because of economics.
- Often when X'ers did move out, they moved in with friends of either gender and with many of them.
- Gen X'ers waited longer than any other generation to get married.

Generation Y - Millennials

- Generation Y is entering the workforce with many of the same constraints as Gen X'ers. They mostly live at home or with groups of friends. Many are just starting careers.
- With the oldest members of Generation Y (those in their early to mid-thirties) entering the housing market, the characteristics of this demanding, strong-willed generation provide many clues to their preferences in living arrangements. For instance, they:
  o Favor the quirky, unique and different.
  o Seek diversity in all aspects of their lives.
  o Prefer urban over suburban environments.
  o Multi-task (One observation: 'Most don't wear watches because watches only do one thing.'" Trisha Riggs, The Ground Floor.

I Gen or Z Gen

● Still live at home for the most part due to age.

Economics

Baby Boomers

● BBer's postponed retirement because of economics which halted the career progressions of Gen X'ers and made entrance into the workforce more difficult for Generation Y.

Generation X

● X'ers faced economic uncertainty their entire lives – recession in the 80's and 2000's, the housing market crash, junk bonds and an ever increasing deficit. X'ers are not doing as well in real terms as the BBer's that came before them.

Generation Y - Millennials

● Entered a volatile job market, with global competition, world crisis, high unemployment and a workforce that wouldn't or couldn't retire.

i Gen or Generation Z

● It's too early to predict how they will or will not affect the economy, but currently there are plenty of openings for them.

Work

Baby Boomers

● BBer's hold power and authority in companies and are motivated by position, perks and prestige. They sacrificed a great deal for work and in some cases their families. Workaholics – they believe younger generations should conform to a culture of overwork. Do not question authority. Believe in face time at the office, and have difficulty adjusting to flexibility trends.

Generational Differences

I worked with a Baby Boomer, hospital CFO who used to say nearly every morning to the Gen X, COO, "Look at Jim coming in late, so he can leave early." Jim was the president of the local youth soccer league and often left early to coach his daughter's team. He might saunter in around 8:30 a.m. Tom was there from 8:00 – 5:00 no matter what – sometimes longer, sometimes earlier, but never less.

Tom, the CFO didn't value his family any less than Jim, (Tom's kids were grown), but the CFO wasn't comfortable not being at work when he was supposed to be. Jim on the other hand, was not going to miss his kid's lives and took a "to hell with it" attitude as he smiled and proceeded to come in late so he could leave early. In between soccer drills Jim checked his phone for issues. He was effectively working.

Priorities shifted from generation to generation. Even though the CFO was joking, he couldn't adapt and really, truly let it go. Jim worked to live rather than lived to work.

Generation X

- They have been laid-off, unemployed, downsized, right-sized and outsourced. They want a balance between work and life and for the first time a generation is, "Working to live, rather than living to work." The example of Jim and Tom above illustrates this point.
- The Social Contract has failed them time and time again.

Generation Y - Millennials

- Generation Y are not afraid to question authority and will sacrifice money and prestige for a better work/life balance.
- Prioritize family over work.
- Value flexibility.

iGen or Z Gen

- More willing to work overtime and do a good job.
- Less likely to have unrealistically high expectations.
- Less rebellious.

Technology

Baby Boomers

- The average age for baby-boomers to start using computers – some still don't know how to use a computer.

Generation X

- Work and technology are intertwined. The average age at which they started using computers was 9.

Generation Y - Millennials

- Many Millennials grew up with technology and rely on it to perform jobs better and for personal entertainment. They would rather text or email than have a face-to face conversation. Work and personal life are intertwined.
- It is who they are.

I Gen or Z Gen

- Super connected to technology – will interrupt a real conversation to attend to a virtual one. The first entire generation to spend their entire childhood with a Smartphone.

Family

Baby Boomers

- Many female Boomers entered the workforce leaving latch key kids – Gen X'ers to fend for themselves after school and on weekends.

Generation X

- Top three signs of a good life – Home, Happy Marriage, and Children.
- In many cases by age 16 they were living in non-traditional families headed by a single parent, or families composed of children from multiple marriages which is probably why family is so important to them. The Jim and Tom example above illustrates this as well.

Generation Y - Millennials

- Prioritize family over work and will work less and make less for a better work/life balance.

iGen or Generation Z

- Slow, deliberate, and protected upbringing. Studies have demonstrated a correlation between mental health (depression) and excessive smartphone usage. They are not being prepared for adulthood adequately. How they will view family is still an unknown due to their age.

*drink beer from boots, (too many guys threw up, and I would have too.)
I watched new guys come out to practice, mostly freshman, looking for a
team, a place to fit in and compete.*

*When the hazing happened, many of the guys never came back. It
wasn't worth it to them. I decided that I was not going to perpetuate an
approach that didn't work. I decided to take a stand against tyranny and
the mistreatment of people to gain acceptance on the team. I removed as
much of the hazing as I could so we could grow as a team and focus on
inclusion. I ended the cycle of subjugation and developed a system that
rewarded people with playing time based on merit. I had the parties at
my house, rather than the bar.*

*We beat Ohio State University at our peak my senior year and many
of us were named to the All Midwest team. It was the first time we beat
OSU since 1972 when the OU Rugby team formed.*

Inherent to Authoritarianism is the **Assumption of Irresponsibility**,
or the assumption that management makes regarding employees; that
they are not competent to make decisions about their work-life when in
reality they are productive, responsible tax-paying parents, spouses and
friends whom make excellent decisions, given the right environment,
daily.

Douglas McGregor's Theory X is a philosophy of management that
is embraced by authoritarian organizations and older generations. It has
been proven ineffective in most modern practice. Management assumes
people are lazy and don't want to work. People interpret Theory X as a
negative set of beliefs about people.

The new way of doing business is called a **Learning Organization**
which embraces flattened hierarchies, teams, employee empowerment,
strategy formulation, and cultural equality. Learning organizations
embrace the **Theory Y** philosophy of management in which management
assumes employees will be ambitious, self-motivated and exercise self-
control. It is believed that employees enjoy mental and physical work
duties. At the heart of this theory is the belief that work is as natural as
play and that each are necessary to be a healthy human being. Employees
possess the ability for creative problem solving, but their talents are
often underused in organizations.

Given the proper conditions, Theory Y managers believe that employees will learn to seek out and accept responsibility, exercise self-control and self-direction in accomplishing objectives to which they are committed. A Theory Y manager believes that, given the right conditions, most people want to do great work. They believe that the satisfaction of doing a good job is a strong motivator. Many people interpret Theory Y as a positive set of beliefs about employees.

*To help us remember, **Theory X** is on the left with the little stick figure refusing to work. **Theory Y** is on the right, with the stick figure exalting the opportunity to work.*

Many of these ideas are difficult for some Baby-Boomer managers to embrace because many were "brought up" under the old, authoritarian approach to leadership which in fact isn't leadership at all. It's management, and very little attention was given to *"The Infinite Space between Management."* Many of the issues managers and employees encounter today are because of authoritarian managers who, prescribe to Theory X clash with employees who need a manager that subscribes to Theory Y and the principles of a learning organization.

Remember, first and foremost it is the leader who must adapt to the changing times, not just the employee.

Characteristics of a Learning Organization – these don't only have to be organizational initiatives, they can also be implemented by each individual leader within their sphere of control.

1. **Company Leadership** has to buy-in to the ideas and practices that make up a learning organization. The first thing is to develop a **flattened hierarchy** which means power and control does not rest solely at the top of the hierarchy. The hierarchy is squished so that if decisions do need to go the top, there are fewer levels to negotiate.

   Leaders don't have to have every answer or solution we just need to be able to facilitate and identify the right answer or solution when the team presents it.

2. **Teams** should be formed to solve problems at a functional level, administrative level and strategic level. If people feel as if they have a say and some control of their work-life and can execute the solutions to problems with their team, they feel a sense of ownership, buy-in and community. They won't want to let their team members down and they tend to self-monitor and motivate one another.

   Small bands of people are created to make big things happen because the strengths of the group overcome the weaknesses of the individual which can be absorbed by the whole.

3. **Employee Empowerment** - Employees must be able to make functional decisions without having to check with someone else. For an employee to feel fully empowered the following characteristics must be present:

   A. **Access to information** – employees want to understand how their piece of the puzzle fits into the overall organizational puzzle. To understand how their piece fits into the organization helps employees find meaning in their work.

To view an entire painting is much more rewarding than viewing just the top right corner. If we want people to think strategically and understand how their role fits into the larger organization we need to give them the tools to see the big picture.

Limited information – Top Right of the Big Picture

The Big Picture

Access to Information

My younger brother sat at the bar in our mother's kitchen when he was 17. She routinely asked us about our lives and dug deeper than he was comfortable with. I was 20 at the time and was much more open to sharing my life with her. I always had been. Regardless, she said to my little brother, "Andy, I heard you have a new girlfriend." He didn't look up from his frozen burrito and said, "Mom, you're on a need to know basis and right now, you don't need to know." She looked at me, I held back my laughter and kind of chuckled because I saw the shock, disappointment and anger on her face. She was not happy. In fact, she was genuinely pissed, but more to the point, her feelings were hurt.

My brother and I will likely see her this holiday season. He'll be 44 and I'll be 47. She'll most likely bring that up and shake her head. In fact, I think it's made her leery to ask either of us too personal of questions to this day.

So, when employees aren't kept in the loop, aren't given access to information and aren't allowed to participate in decisions, are minimized/

marginalized, expect long-term negative repercussions which will likely take the form of decreased participation and stifled innovation.

B. **Accountability** – employees, if given the right tools, guidelines and freedom to find success, will find success and even monitor and control their own success.

*Being accountable to one's self, based on
organizational goals and guidelines,
is the strongest, most lasting motivation toward success.*

C. **Participation** – employees do not want to feel that decisions are made for them, but by them, and with their input.

*"When you have a problem, ask your employees for the
solution…time after time I have seen businesses struggle when
the solutions to problems were known by employees."*
(Jack Shewmaker, former President of Wal-Mart)

D. **Innovation** - employees need to be encouraged to try new ideas, processes and ways of doing business. This means that there has to be tolerance for trial and error. So often we expect perfection the first time.

Innovation

*Thomas Edison developed over 1000 light bulbs that
didn't work. Thank goodness he had the spirit of
innovation and didn't get discouraged by failure.*

It is with each failure that our focus on success becomes more acute.

"What made you successful in the past, won't in the future."
(Lew Platt, Hewlett Packard CEO and founder)

4. **Strategy Formulation** – employees should be asked for input to develop strategies for success. This also helps gain buy-in from employees when it becomes time to implement the strategy.

If they would just ask me, I could tell them what needs done.

5. **Cultural Equality** – employees at all levels should be treated equally and fairly. There should not be a hierarchy that exists where one person is more important to the team than another. In healthcare for example, this discrepancy occurs between caregivers.

Nursing Units and Cultural Equality

The duties that a Registered Nurse (RN) performs as compared to a Licensed Practical Nurse (LPN) as compared to a Patient Care Assistant (PCA) are very different, and have different value. Yet, each position depends on the other and neither can do their job without the other. Each member of the team has equal importance and they should be consulted, and given a say in each decision as it relates to their work environment. A change in an RN's role will have an impact on a PCA's role. To make a change in the RN's role without consulting the PCA to see how the change will affect them is a complete disregard for what they contribute.

Each person on the team has a job to do for the success of the team. Those jobs are valued differently, and paid accordingly, but that isn't what is important, what is, is that no one can do their job without the other, so under this model, importance is equal, value or pay is different, but at no time, can one do their job without the assistance of another. If one fails, they all fail.

A car must have an engine, drive shaft, wheels,
steering wheel and driver to be effective.
An engine is useless without a drive shaft to turn the wheels.

Wheels are useless without a steering wheel to guide them.
The steering wheel is useless without a driver to direct the car.

The Leaders Role in Employee Development – Maslow's Needs Hierarchy of Motivation

Abraham Maslow along with Carl Rogers are the two people identified with founding Humanistic Psychology. My bachelor's degree is in psychology and because of these two, I would classify myself as a Humanist. We focus on the good in people and believe that everyone wants to be great if given an environment to excel. Humanistic psychologists believe that: An individual's behavior is primarily determined by their perception of the world around them.

- Individuals are not solely the product of their environment.
- Individuals are internally directed and motivated to fulfill their human potential.
- They focus on the positive potential of human beings.

Humanists believe that a leader's primary role is to grow people by developing their skills, abilities and knowledge, but not only that, preparing them to lead in their own right. It is through teaching and training that employees prepare for greater responsibility. It is the leader's job to keep employees intellectually stimulated and always reaching for a higher goal. They focus on filling *"the Infinite Space between Management and Skill Set"* with inspiration.

Stagnation breeds discontent and decay, and
challenge breeds' responsibility and growth.

The pyramid below illustrates the most primal needs at the bottom and then the more advanced needs toward the tip of the pyramid. The key to understanding the needs hierarchy as described by Maslow is that a lower level need must be obtained prior to a higher level need even being considered because it's wasted time and frankly impossible.

One is not concerned with their self-esteem if they are sitting in the rain, starving and thirsty.

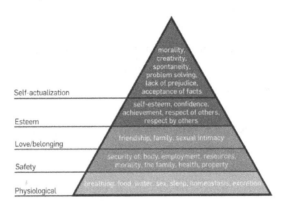

A leader's primary focus is to inspire greatness.

Needs Hierarchy as related to Work – The Leader's Role

Physiological Needs – Obtaining employment will provide shelter, food and water. Sex will need to be found outside of work. But frankly, the likelihood is greater if we have jobs.

Safety Needs – Employment will provide a means to maintaining food and shelter on an on-going basis and the result is that safety is satisfied.

Social Needs – Employment is a venue for establishing social networks and friends.

Self-Esteem Needs – Mutually valuable and respectful relationships between the employee and leadership will foster achievement, recognition and respect from others. This is the level a leader can have a positive effect on an employee's perception of themselves and the organization. If employees feel good about themselves, they feel better about work.

Self-Actualization Needs – It should be the goal of all leaders to make their employees the best they can be and then encourage them to move into another more challenging role or project. This is the most dynamic aspect of the needs hierarchy and it can change over time as a person grows and develops. The goal is to keep employees at the self-esteem level, and always striving to be the best they can be through self-actualization. This will make for productive, engaged and long-term employees. There isn't a blueprint to self-actualization, each person is different. Good leadership, through discussions with employees will help each employee set a course to self-actualization, reach it and move onto the next challenge. It is everything we do as a leader, in *the Infinite Space between Management and Skill Set* that helps people grow, and gives them confidence.

Maslow's Needs Hierarchy

*You're on a plane. It crashes. Everyone dies but you. You find yourself washed up on a beach. Think Tom Hanks in Castaway, The Lord of the Flies from middle school and Dances with Wolves. The first thing you'll do is scope the island. It's uninhabited. The next thing you'll do is locate water, food and build a shelter – **Physiological needs**.*

*The next thing you'll do is ensure your safety. You'll secure your resources, stabilize your shelter and ensure you are able to rest safely – **Safety needs**. Next, you'll create a social sphere. "Wilson" in Castaway.*

*But maybe you hear what seems to be human noise coming from a nearby island. You can't help yourself and you devise a scheme to get to the other island – **Social needs**. Why? We as humans need interaction with others. We are tribal creatures. We thrive in groups or teams.*

*So, you meet these folks, they are indigenous and lost to time, but still you want to integrate into their culture – think Dances with Wolves when Kevin Costner's character integrates with the Native Americans. Why? We all need to find a place, our place, given our own circumstances. You develop esteem through your interactions with these people because you are able to show them new ways to do ordinary tasks from your time on the mainland - **Self-esteem** needs.*

*Now, all you want is to be the best you can at some aspect of tribal, island life. You long for and must be the best you can be – **Self-actualization needs**.*

In Conclusion

As leaders, our job is to remove roadblocks so people can operate at their highest level. Sometimes this means training them and sometimes this means giving them room to grow. It may mean they need to be challenged, pushed and guided. Remember, each person is different and are at different levels within the hierarchy. Be aware of what they need and give it to them so they are prepared to give you what you need. Fill *"The Infinite Space between Management and Skill Set,"* with what they need, not what you think they need if you want them to be great and excel.

CHAPTER 3

ENHANCED COMMUNICATION

A Brief Communication Overview

Talking to you is like clapping with one hand.

THE SENTENCE ABOVE IS TOO often how conversations go in our world. With one hand, no sound is emitted, therefore clapping has not occurred. Communication is no different, it takes two parties to communicate – one must send a message and at least one person must receive the message. Simply hearing the message is considerably different than listening and understanding the message. In all cases, each person that hears a message perceives different meaning.

"Meaning is in the mind." (*Lesikar, Flately,* 13)

This creates an inconsistency in the message sent and the message received and then an even deeper inconsistency is created if there are multiple people receiving the same message.

Our goal is to minimize inconsistency and enhance the communication process.

Communication is a dynamic process with many levels and layers of understanding. For a message to be received and understood there has to be a sender and a receiver. For successful communication, the receiver has to understand and comprehend the sender's intent.

For example, if you picked up the phone and on the other end a voice spoke Russian to you, and you didn't speak Russian, communication would not have occurred. Although you would likely be able to understand some aspect of the message through tone of voice, cadence and intensity, etc. The communication process is outlined below.

The Process of Human Communication

1. **A Message is Sent** – this begins the process of communication. Someone conceptualizes a message and speaks it.
2. **Sensory World** – a message must enter the receiver's sensory world – hearing, smell, taste, touch, sight.
3. **Detection** – the message is detected through stimulation of the senses and the main consideration at this point in the communication process is how acutely tuned in to the message the receiver is. Is it actually stimulating or is it "white noise?"

In one ear and right out the other.

4. **Filtering** – the message has entered the sensory world and has been detected, now it is filtered by everything the receiver has done, heard, seen, touched, and experienced in their lifetime. Meaning is assigned to the message as it relates to the receiver's reference points. This is the point in which miscommunication occurs.

Everyone has different life experiences; therefore everyone takes different meaning from every message. The goal is to be clear and concise in your message so we leave no room for unintended interpretation of our message.

5. **Response Formation** – if the message was received and meaning was given to the message in a sufficiently strong way, a response will be developed. This is the most complex aspect of communication.

"There is evidence that the ability to respond meaningfully, is related to one's intelligence and the extent that one permits the mind to react. The ability to evaluate filtered information and formulate meaning also is related to language ability." (*Lesikar, Flately,* 11)

Non-Verbal and Verbal Communication

There are two main avenues by which people communicate face-to-face – Non-Verbal and Verbal Communications. Research indicates that 85% of communication is conveyed through non-verbal cues during a face-to-face conversation, such as tone of voice, posture, body language and facial expressions. This means that verbal communication represents only 15% of the message we convey during an oral communication. **Verbal Communication**, the words used in communication have meaning in definitional form.

Tone of Voice

It is difficult to misinterpret the word, "Dog." Generally, without seeing the person say the word, you conjure an image of a dog – probably your dog if you have one. You would have some idea how the person felt about dogs, just by hearing the word dog. But what if you saw and heard someone say, "Dog," in a high pitched voice, and leaned down to the dog with their hands on their knees and smiled? You may get the point that they are very fond of the dog.

Non-Verbal Communication is the way we present words through **body language, space, time and paralanguage**. It is where 85% of the message is communicated. These are non-verbal cues and these cues can indicate a positive or negative intent to the message and can indicate truth, lies, apprehension and in fact, every other human emotion. People are very keen when it comes to understanding non-verbal cues. They may not be able to verbalize the understanding, but it is there, deep in their minds. Through the millennia we've become master sensors of human interaction.

Non-verbal communication is the most ancient form of human communication. We intuit and perceive the true meaning of a message through body language. We just need to trust it.

Amy Cuddy is a Social Psychologist and Associate Professor in the Negotiations, Organizations and Markets Unit at the Harvard Business School. She has proven through her research that our body language can be used to change who we are. If we take a certain posture, hormone levels actually change and convince our minds that we are more confident and powerful. Thereby, enhancing how we behave and ultimately changing the outcomes for the better just through changing how we present ourselves.

Amy Cuddy – *"Your Body Language Shapes Who You Are"*
http://www.ted.com/talks/lang/en/amy_cuddy_your_body_language_shapes_who_you_are.html

"Our non-verbals govern how we think and feel about ourselves." (Amy Cuddy)

*"Our bodies change our minds
...and our minds change our behavior
...and our behavior changes our outcomes."* (Amy Cuddy)

If body language is so powerful, as Amy Cuddy illustrated through her research, wouldn't it be wonderful if we were able to use this not only to our advantage, but to the advantage of everyone around us?

Do not underestimate the power of non-verbal communication. Use it to help you communicate better, effect change positively, and increase the satisfaction you and others obtain from work.

Body Language – When we wave our arms or fingers, wrinkle our foreheads, stand erect, smile, gaze at another, and so on, we convey certain meanings. In particular, the face and eyes, gestures, posture, and physical appearance reflect the inner workings of emotions in our bodies. (*Lesikar, Flatley,* 409)

A picture is worth a thousand words.

Body Language Tells the Story

We've all either been in or have seen the situation I'm going to describe. You're in your car and you pull up to a stop light. Next to you, a car wobbles back and forth. You look closer and the woman in the driver seat is pounding her hand on the steering wheel. She's yelling at a man in the passenger seat. You can't make out the words.

Do we need to know what she is saying to get the meaning of her message? Let's take a poll, is she saying, "Baby, I love you so much I can't stand it? Or is she so pissed that it doesn't matter what she's saying, you just know you're glad you're not in the car and that other guy is. The point is, you don't need to hear the words to know that she "is mad as hell, and she's not going to take it, anymore." (Excerpt from the speech given by Actor Peter Finch, playing Howard Beale in the Movie, *Network*)

Space Language– the space between two people can indicate how comfortable they are with each other, how much they trust one another and in fact space language communicates just like body language. Many experts agree that there are four different types of space:

It is uncomfortable if the space people share is not agreed upon.

Kramer from the TV show "*Seinfeld,*" meets
the 'close talker' - Link below.
https://www.youtube.com/watch?v=Ipeh0WFAnhc

1. **Intimate** - Physical Contact – 18 inches
2. **Personal** – 18 inches – 4 feet

3. **Social** – 4 feet – 12 feet
4. **Public** – 12 feet to the range of seeing or hearing

Time Language - communicates to people in how you respond to appointments, requests, meetings, and whether or not you respect another's time. When time is shared by people and one party's time is not respected, a clear, negative non-verbal cue is being sent.

You can wait. Don't you know my time is more important than yours...
or worse, you are insignificant?

Paralanguage – is the way words are said and emphasized. Paralanguage is closest to communication with words because it is how certain words are said or emphasized. Read the examples below and emphasize the underlined words to illustrate the differences in meaning of each sentence even though the same words are used.

"You put the wrong **em 'PHA sis** *on the* wrong **syl 'LA ble**.*"*
(Mike Meyers, *"A View from the Top"* - Link below
https://www.youtube.com/watch?v=fbjE8KI-
j3M&feature=em-share_video_user

You communicate well with me. You communicate well with me. You communicate well with me. You communicate well with me.

Take a look at the additional scenarios below as an example as to how the same words can have two totally different meanings given the body language that is exhibited.

Non-Verbal Cues

Negative Non-Verbal Cues

Jane stood with her hands on her hips and glared at Jack. Her eyebrows were furrowed and all her weight rested on her left leg. Her right foot pointed out and away.

Jack said, *"It's how you look at me, that makes me feel this way."*

Her head tilted sideways. Her eyes opened wide and she looked upward. Her palms flipped to the sky and her arms stretched outward. She said, "Yeah, I'm sure you're right, Jack."

> *"It wasn't what she said that made him mad;*
> *it was how she said it."*

Positive Non-Verbal Cues

Jane stood with her hands loosely clasped in front of her. She faced Jack and both feet pointed directly at him. Her posture was straight and she gazed into Jack's eyes.

Jack said, "It's the way you look at me that makes me feel this way."

A smile crossed her face and she focused deeper into Jack's eyes. She nodded her head unconsciously and slow. She said, "Yeah, I'm sure you're right, Jack."

> *"It wasn't what she said that made him like her;*
> *it was how she said it."*

The same words, yet totally different meaning based on body language.

Non-Verbal Cues

My wife used to say to me, "it's not what you said, it's how you said it," I would say, (like an idiot) "Well, don't look at my body, face and expressions. Listen to the words I'm saying!"

It didn't matter, there was no hiding the frustration I felt no matter how calculated my words were. Eventually I learned I was not only lying to myself, but I was trying to get her to believe the lie that my body language could not hide. I had to make sure my body language mirrored the words coming from my mouth. If I couldn't, there was no point in speaking.

Our body language fills "the Infinite Space between" words and gives the real meaning of the message. Make sure the non-spoken message is consistent with the verbal message you want to send. If they don't it is either sarcastic or hypocritical and neither are received well in heated moments.

Verbal Communication

The key to increasing communication effectiveness is to ensure verbal cues and non-verbal cues are aligned. If there is inconsistency, it may leave the listener befuddled. Sarcasm is an example that is often sent through inconsistent verbal and non-verbal messages. The words do not align with the tone of the voice and poor word choice can lead the listener to a negative conclusion. The same message can either be conveyed positively or negatively. It is a matter of word choice.

Negative Word Choice	Positive Word Choice
We have a **problem** with the project.	We've run into some **challenges** with the project.
The sub **didn't** show up today and he's coming in **way over** budget.	The sub we chose had an **unforeseen issue** today and the original budget projections were **light**.
Your performance is **terrible**. You **don't** come close to our expectations. You **can't** expect us to continue to pay you for **poor** work.	We'd like to see your performance **improve**. We need you to hold your end of the **deal** so we can ensure you are paid for the work we **agreed** to.

Taking a moment to communicate with positive words takes a bit longer, but the reward is that you may be able to keep a client or employee from becoming irritated, threatened or scared. But most importantly, if you invest time and energy on the front-end, the back-end runs smoother.

Positive and Negative Communication Styles

People either learn to communicate or choose to communicate with certain styles. There is evidence that behaviors may not reflect a person's "traits or personality," so much as they reflect the situations in which people find themselves. *(Myers, Myers, 97-98.)*

This is similar to the idea of **contingent leadership** which we will discuss in the next chapter. The situation determines how we behave and our behavior in a certain situation determines the outcome and the outcome determines the success of the situation. Contingency Leadership is critical to understand so that each situation is seen as unique. What worked in one seemingly similar situation won't always work in others. We need to take in all the factors available to us and develop an individual plan, not a canned response from the past.

People tend to use different styles to accomplish their own initiatives or agendas. Often we employ a negative communication style when our arguments are not strong. This alienates people and leaves them feeling as if they have been taken advantage of, insulted or demeaned. Remember, particularly the up and coming generations prefer a participative style of leadership in which their voices are heard, they are given an opportunity to ask questions and also seek clarification.

The younger generation wants to know the "why" behind the requests made of them. Hell, everyone does!

If an employee is given a say in the process and their ideas or input are not only heard but considered and possibly incorporated, the likelihood of gaining buy-in from them has increased tremendously.

If in business, the goals of the leader are aligned with the goals of the employee there is no good reason not to sincerely ask an employee's opinion on what should be done and how it should be done. Remember, the leader doesn't have to have all the answers; they just need to recognize a better solution when it is presented. The most effective way to do this is to use the assertive style of communication as illustrated below. The negative communication styles that leave employees feeling used and abused are illustrated so that you may understand them and avoid them.

In this table, the question could be almost anything. Assume for this example, that the question is; "What movie should we go see?"

Style	Statement	Translation	Approach
Aggressive	"Only one movie in town is any good We'll go to that one."	"My way or nothing.	Negative
Placating -	"Whatever movie you want to see is fine with me."	"Poor dumb me; I'm really helpless, and have no idea."	Negative
Intellectual -	"Reviews say that the new French film is directed, acted and filmed well, and is a "must."	"I have no feelings about it myself, only the intellectual advice from others."	Neutral
Manipulative -	"I'm not sure I want to go to a movie."	Coax me; I want to be in a position of deciding by playing hard-to-get.	Negative
Assertive -	"I'm most interested in the new Robert Redford movie. How about you?	"Here's what I want. What do you want?" *(Myers, Myers 98)*	Positive

An assertive communicator is confident and open to other's ideas. It isn't about being right; it is about sharing one's perspective and then listening to another's perspective. Generally, somewhere in the middle lies the best solution for both parties.

Listening

Talking to you is like clapping with one hand.

Most of us have felt ignored by our co-workers, friends, spouses and others. Then, other times we feel like these same people, "just get us." Think about the times when you felt ignored and then think about the times you felt syncopation. What were the differences? Most likely it was that the person you were talking to actively listened to you. Not having someone listen to you, especially a manager or supervisor, leaves the employee feeling unappreciated, undervalued, and ignored. These feelings lead to increased turnover in work life… and divorce in personal life.

The most underrated communication skill is **listening**. Most people want to talk and while they are in the middle of a conversation are, instead of listening, gearing up for what they are going to say in rebuttal. There are public speaking courses in universities, but there are few if any improved listening courses. Some research suggests that we only listen with 25% effectiveness. *(Guffey,* 4). What is the point of improving speaking skills if no one is going to listen anyway? The improvement isn't needed in the message. It's needed in the listener. With 25% listening effectiveness this creates a tremendous opportunity for large improvements in communication.

There are two main ways people listen. One is easy and the other is hard and much effort has to be exerted for effectiveness. This is fundamentally why people are poor listeners. We want to talk rather than listen. **Passive Listening** and **Active Listening** are two wildly different ideas.

"Listening is one of the best gifts you can give someone, and it's free."

Passive Listening is what you would do if you wanted to make your employees feel undervalued, underappreciated and frustrated.

Passive Listening

Passive listening is what you do when there is a radio in the background of your home, or car. You hear it, but you are not exactly absorbing the lyrics and certainly not the meaning of the lyrics.

If you are a parent, you know what passive listening looks like. It is the look your child gives you when they have done something they shouldn't have. They nod their head at you and kind of look around sadly and jiggle something in their hands. Many of you have probably seen this phenomenon and asked your child, "What did I just say?" The child is then snapped back into reality and the glaze over their eyes clears and they look like a bright-eyed child again, at least for another ten seconds.

If they were listening with purpose, they would be able to rattle off what your message to them was, "DON'T THROW ROCKS AT YOUR BROTHER!" So instead, you have to say it again and refocus their attention on what you are trying to communicate. The difference between a nine year old and a thirty-nine year old is thirty years, but why isn't there thirty years of improvement in the ability to listen?

It's hard work to be a good listener. You must decide to do it.

As a manager, you should avoid passive listening at all costs. The price you will pay is tremendous as it relates to loss of trust, respect, and buy-in. Employees are aware when they are not being listened to – they see the haze over your eyes, like the glaze on a donut. The goal is to be an **active listener.**

Active listeners participate in the communication process.
They take an interest in the communicator, the message,
the meaning of the message, and they shut up.

Active Listening

The list below was developed by an anonymous author, and has been cited and quoted many times in many different venues over the years.

The longer one listens attentively, the more power
our words have when we do speak.

The Ten Commandments of Active Listening

1. **Stop Talking** – Unfortunately, most of us prefer talking to listening. Even when we are not talking, we are inclined to concentrate on what to say next rather than on listening to others. You must stop talking before you can listen.
2. **Put the Speaker at Ease** – If you make the speaker feel at ease, he or she will do a better job of talking. Then you will have better input to work with.
3. **Show the Speaker You Want to Listen** – If the speaker sees you are listening to understand, rather than oppose, you will create a climate for information exchange. You should look interested and be interested. Doing things like reading, looking at your watch, checking your smart phone and looking away distracts the speaker.
4. **Remove Distractions** – The things you do also can distract the speaker. So don't doodle, tap with your pencil, shuffle papers or the like.

5. **Empathize with the Speaker-** If you place yourself in the speaker's position and look at things from the speaker's point of view, you will help create a climate of understanding that can result in a true exchange of information.

6. **Be Patient** – You will need to allow the speaker plenty of time. Remember, not everyone can get to the point as quickly and clearly as you. Do not interrupt. Interruptions are barriers to the exchange of information.

7. **Hold Your Temper** – From our knowledge of the workings of our minds we know that anger impedes communication. Angry people build walls between each other. They harden their position and block their minds to the words of others.

8. **Go Easy on Argument and Criticism** – Argument and criticism tend to put the speaker on the defensive. He or she then tends to "clam up" or get angry. Thus, even if you win the argument, you lose. Rarely does either party benefit from argument and criticism.

9. **Ask Questions** – By frequently asking questions, you display an open mind and show that you are listening and thereby assist the speaker in developing his or her message and in improving the correctness of meaning.

10. **STOP TALKING** – The last commandment is to stop talking. It was also the first. All the other commandments depend on it. (Lesikar, Flately, 407)

You must know the other person's viewpoint
before you can respond intelligently.

Additional Tips for Active Listening

Provide Verbal Feedback
1. Ask relevant questions at appropriate times. These should be few and far between.
2. Allow the person to know you are listening, by giving a simple, "uh-huh, OK, or right."

3. Saying, "I understand" goes a long way in getting people to be open. It doesn't mean you agree. It just means you hear and understand what they are saying.

Non-Verbal Affirmation of Listening – This is what you can do to let people know you are hearing them and actively listening without saying a word.

1. Nod your head in the affirmative
2. Maintain eye contact, but do not stare – that's creepy.
3. Present yourself with open posture
   A. Face the person
   B. Smile
      The Hidden Power of Smiling – A Ted Talk from Ron Gutman demonstrates how we all have a hidden superpower within us that makes or gives us:
      - A Universal Language
      - Live Longer
      - Our brains feel like we've eaten 2000 bars of chocolate
      - Our brains feel like we've received $25,000
      - Appear more likable, courteous and competent
      - The ability to overcome a frown from others
      - Appear more attractive to others
      https://www.ted.com/talks/ron_gutman_the_hidden_power_of_smiling

   C. Do not cross your arms
   D. Do not tap your foot or hand – this indicates impatience.

Shut up and Listen

When my wife and I first were married, we moved to Colorado to start our life together without our old friends and family. We wanted to be alone, you know, together. This put a lot of pressure on me to be her go to person when things were bad at work, when things were good at work, when she had a thought and wanted to share it, when she was happy, when she was sad...You get the picture.

She came home from work each day and downloaded all the issues she had with her employees, to me. Me, having recently been a grad school graduate in the fine art of Human Resources Management, launched into solving her employee problems. I cut her off, started spieling theories, what I would do, how to get them to do what she wanted them to do, and so on. I had all the answers. She didn't think so. Her body language sagged, her demeanor became distant and I didn't understand why.

Why was she telling me this if she didn't want help? She informed me that she did not want me to solve her problems. I couldn't understand why she wanted to tell me about her problems and not solve them. We argued. She finally said, "I don't want you to solve my problems, I just want you to listen to them."

It took me a little while to fully grasp this and still to this day, I feel a little useless when she tells me about her day, employee problems, and I sit and do nothing. I do nothing! But what I realized was that my life got much easier; all I had to do was sit back, nod my head and ask, "Well, what'd you do?" Nod some more, grunt, say, "uh, huh," and then she would stop talking, she would thank me, and we would move onto the next thing in life. The epiphany that she helped me realize also became the day I began to learn.

To learn and to help, we must listen.

Shut up and Listen - II

This situation occurred at the same hospital that Tom, the Baby-Boomer CFO, Jim the Gen X'er COO and I worked. Her name was Gloria, but everyone called her Big G. She was the Emergency Department Director. They called her Big G because she had a huge personality, she was excitable and was very outspoken about the quality of care people were supposed to receive, but often didn't receive due to space issues.

We were a Trauma center. There were 300 beds in the hospital, which were nearly always at capacity. The ER overflowed and patients were often triaged in the hallways. I had been with the hospital as the Head of

HR for about two months. I wanted to make an impact and improve the lives of our employees, leaders and consequently, the patients.

Big G came into my office on fire, like someone had poured gasoline on her and lit a match. She stood over my desk, and vehemently explained six different issues at once. I couldn't follow her or make connections between the issues she jumped back and forth from. I asked questions and with each question, she grew more exasperated. The pitch of her voice went higher, her eye brows narrowed and she looked at me like I lobbed grenades at her with each question. Five minutes into the discussion, she left in a flurry, just like she came in. Needless to say, the conversation didn't go well. She left in worse shape than when she came in.

I sat back and contemplated where I had failed her. I decided that if a similar situation was ever to occur again, I would say as few words as possible. I remembered what Amy, my wife, had told me when we were first married.

A couple months later, the ER overflowed. Gloria stormed into my office like a wildfire. I leaned back in my chair, crossed my leg, sat attentively and made eye contact with her. I nodded and said, "uh huh." "What did you do?" "Then what?" "I understand." I may have said 20 words if you count a few grunts of empathy and understanding. This went on for about ten minutes. She ranted and raved and flailed her arms. I had no idea what she was talking about.

She stopped dead in her tracks, in the middle of a thought, and slammed both hands on my desk. She pointed her finger directly in my face and said, "Thanks, Matt. This was great!" She turned and jogged back to the ER. She didn't want me to solve her problems, she didn't want me to do anything. She just needed a place and an ear to vent. She needed to talk through the problem as she thought it through. To this day, I still do not know what the problem or solution was that day, but I know that I helped Gloria come to it, by doing one thing – listening...actively. Sometimes, the Infinite Space between can be filled with silence.

Patterns of Communication – Giving Good and Bad News – Verbal and Written

In your role as manager, you may be called upon to write memos, letters or other forms of communication in addition to just speaking. There are two different approaches to developing your message both orally and written. The approach depends on how the information you are sharing is intended to be received.

To put it in a nutshell, it depends on whether the message is positive or negative. The **direct pattern** of communication is used for good or neutral messages and the **indirect pattern** is used for negative or persuasive messages.

The direct and indirect patterns of communication can be used in written and verbal messages. Below you will see examples of direct and indirect communication styles.

Direct Pattern of Communication - (for Good News and Neutral News)

A. **Begin with the Objective** – If you are seeking information, start asking for it. If you are sharing good news, say it.
B. **Present a Necessary Explanation** – Explain why you are requesting the information or why the news is good.
C. **End with a Goodwill Statement** – End the communication with a statement of goodwill because this is normally how friendly people handle these situations. (*Lesiker, Flately,* 100-101)

Example - **The Direct Pattern** –you are telling someone they are being promoted.

Begin with the Objective
"Congratulations, you got the promotion you applied for."
Necessary Explanation
"There were a lot of applicants, but your experience, innovation, and longevity set you apart."
Goodwill Statement

"This is a terrific honor and I know you'll
be great. Thanks for applying."

Indirect Pattern of Communication – (For Bad News, Proposals, Persuasive Messages, or Refusals)

A. **Begin with a Strategic Buffer** – Use words that set up the strategy to overcome or reduce the impact of the negative message that follows.

B. **Develop a Strategy** – Make this as logical and convincing as you can. Use words and reasoning that emphasize the reader's viewpoint. You are going to want to **"Answer the Why"** in this section of the communication strategy.

C. **Present the Bad News Positively** – After you have buffered the bad news, try to understand the reader's viewpoint, minimize a negative response and give the bad news as positively as possible.

D. **End with a Positive Note** – Even a skillfully crafted bad news presentation is likely to put the reader in an unhappy frame of mind; you should end the message with a happy or positive note. Your goal is to shift the person's thoughts to happier things. (Lesiker, Flately, 101-102)

<u>Example -</u> **The Indirect Pattern** – you must tell someone they are not going to be promoted.

Strategic Buffer
"A lot of qualified people applied for this position.
Strategy Development
"Many of them had excellent skills and some differentiated themselves because of their longevity, creativity, innovation and specific experience to the needs of the position."
Presenting the Bad News Positively
"There will be a time when you are the most qualified person for this position, but at this time however, someone else was more qualified."
Ending with a Positive Note

"Keep working hard and gaining experience and if you ever have questions or need clarification on anything, please let me know."

The key to good communication is to understand what it looks and sounds like, and then practice it. It isn't easy for most people or the statistics would be different.

Good communication is the single most
cited reason for business success.

In Conclusion

It isn't technical knowledge or education that makes for good communication; it is whether or not people can communicate accurately, openly, concisely and with mutual respect. The simple act of listening actively illustrates concern, interest and the desire to understand the employee's perspective. It makes people feel valued, and valued employees are good, productive, engaged employees.

If we know that 85% of communication is conveyed through body language and 25% of the words we speak are actually heard, then…we have a tremendous opportunity to improve in what research calls the most important business skill – communication, and more importantly the most important communication skill - listening - by 96.25%. 15% x 25% = **3.75%** of what is said is conveyed through the spoken word. The rest is through the other language modes. Focus! Fill the *Infinite Space between Management and Skill Set* with your sincere desire to listen, encourage and help people be great.

CHAPTER 4

MOTIVATION

Overview on Motivation

"A creative man is motivated by the desire to achieve,
not by the desire to beat others." (Ayn Rand)

"I do not try to dance better than anyone else,
I only try to dance better than myself." (Mikhail Baryshnikov)

FOR THE MOST PART, WE can thank motivation for all the wonderful creations, innovations, and good in the world, not to mention the perpetuation of human beings. Most of the incredible things we have or enjoy are derived from the desire to make things better not only for ourselves but for others and, specifically, the greater good. When people do things with the right motivation, magnificent things result. **Motivation** is an inner drive that directs a person's behavior toward goals. A **goal** is the satisfaction of a need, and a **need** is the difference between a desired state and an actual state.

Motivation can also wreak havoc if it is from a place of suboptimum balance, such as the desire to dominate, gain power, or to receive accolades for performing well. This motivation created the atomic bomb, the nuclear bomb, unethical behavior and is also responsible for those people in the workplace who just can't seem to find peace in their work or with the work of others. No matter what, they find something wrong with their environment, the work itself or the people around them. Often, it's because they just can't seem to be positive. They errantly feel that they are in need of external factors to satisfy the discrepancy between what they need internally and what they are getting and what they desire externally and what they get. These two main types of motivation are intrinsic and extrinsic.

Intrinsic Motivation calls people to action from an internal need to fulfill some outcome for personal satisfaction such as being all they can be, and helping another person from a place of benevolence. It is a desire to be effective and to perform a behavior for its own sake, (Myers, 473) because they enjoy it and gain satisfaction from it. This is deep satisfaction and long lasting.

Intrinsic motivation provides a satisfaction that propels people, feeds their soul and sustains their inner ambition and drive.

Extrinsic Motivation – calls people to action from an external need to fulfill some outcome, such as money, power, prestige or notoriety. It is seeking external rewards and avoiding punishments. (Myers, 473) It is a desire to be noticed, to gain attention or obtain material objects.

Extrinsic Motivation provides fleeting satisfaction that ultimately leaves one feeling empty and striving to fill an ever increasing and insatiable desire for more.

When a person does something because they expect some external validation or reward they are selling themselves short and will never reach self-actualization as Maslow describes it. They sell themselves short because they are not doing what they need to do to fulfill their own internal needs and desires for satisfaction. They fall short because no external validation or reward can surpass or supplant the satisfaction that is derived from doing something because it is what one simply has to do, for themselves.

It is difficult to take care of others and to be liked by others, when one does not take care of and like themselves.

Caring for One's Self to Help Others

Consider what flight attendants tell us before each flight. "Remove the oxygen mask from the overhead and secure it around your head, first. Then help others if necessary." They say this because if you are passed out on the ground, you are useless to everyone. You must take care of yourself before you can help others, otherwise you are useless to them.

A study done by Janet Spence and Robert Helmreich in 1983 concluded that intrinsic motivation produces high achievement and that extrinsic motivation (such as the desire for a high paying career) often does not. Spence and Helmreich identified and assessed three facets of motivation:

1. **People's quests for mastery** (as shown, for example, by their strongly agreeing that "if I am not good at something I would rather keep struggling to master it than move on to something I may be good at"); - Intrinsic
2. **Their drive to work** ("I like to work hard.") - Intrinsic
3. **Their competitiveness** ("I really enjoy working in situations involving skill and competition.) – Extrinsic

"Despite similar abilities, people oriented toward mastery and hard work typically achieve more. If students, they get better grades; if MBA graduates, they earn more money: if scientists, their work is more often cited by other scientists. No surprise there. But, surprisingly in Spence and Helmreich's studies those who were most competitive (which is a more extrinsic orientation) often achieved less." (Myers, 373)

Employee motivation effects productivity, and part of a manager's job is to channel motivation toward the accomplishment of organizational goals. The study of motivation helps managers understand what prompts people to initiate action, what influences their choice of action and why they persist in that action over time. (Daft, Marcic, 410) It not only affects productivity but it affects how they perceive their environment, their morale, and their confidence and resolve to do what is right.

As leaders we want people who are "in it" for the right reasons. We want carpenters who *must* build and are attracted to creation, not to the money, and we want doctors who have an immense desire to cure and make life better, rather than seek the prestige that comes from being a doctor.

For leaders to surround themselves with people who are intrinsically motivated is a tremendous step toward success. However, this is not exactly practical. So, what we are left with as leaders is a need to understand what motivates people. The following pages will describe various theories of motivation and shed light on the reasons people feel motivated, and the reasons they feel unmotivated. What motivates one person is going to be different than what motivates others. Leaders study *the Infinite Space between Management and Skill Sets* or in other words an employee's actions to understand what drives them.

11 Perspectives on Motivational Theory and Work

1. **Goal Setting Theory** is a motivational theory which states that people have conscious goals that energize them and direct their thoughts and behaviors toward one end. (Bateman, Snell, 413) People can use goals to guide their behavior and steer them to a mutually rewarding end for the organization and themselves. To do this there are a few factors that must be in place for goals to be effective:

    A. **The goal must be acceptable to the employee** - goals must not conflict with the employee's values and there should be a reason for the person to pursue those goals. Mutual goal development is a key component to developing acceptable goals that people want to strive for. Goals are much more effective if the person trying to reach the goal has helped develop the goal rather than that goal being handed to them by someone else;

    B. **Challenging yet attainable** – goals should push and inspire people to improve performance but, as we'll learn later with the expectancy theory of motivation, if the expectation of attaining the goal is unrealistic, motivation suffers significantly and can even work against the attainment of goals;

C. **Specific, quantifiable, and measurable** – if an employee can see that they have reached their goal, the feeling of satisfaction is greater. The attainment of a goal should be finite and definitive. It is like painting a wall and stepping back, nodding your head and saying, "That looks good. I did a good job." It helps to know when success has been attained or when it is still pending.

Ambiguity leads to uncertainty and uncertainty leads to assumptions, and assumptions lead to negativity.

Reaching a goal is validation for hard work and inspiration to go after the next goal.

Goals and plans help employees identify with the organization and motivate them by reducing uncertainty and clarifying **what** should be accomplished. Lack of a clear goal can damage employee motivation and commitment. Whereas a goal provides the **why** of an organization or subunit's existence, a plan tells the **how.** (Daft, Marcic, 140) Each functional unit of an organization can develop their own goals so employees can understand why they are doing what they are doing. Of course each functional goal, should drive toward the organizational goals.

It is even advisable to develop these goals and plans as a group. Identify the "why", "how" and "what," of what you do. These can act as a beacon for you and your employees to keep everyone focused and from crashing into the rocky shoreline. It will also establish what you believe as a group and it will allow each person to monitor their behavior as it relates to reaching the goal.

The Golden Circle as Related to Goal Setting and Motivation

Simon Sinek works for the RAND Corporation as an adjunct staff member and advises on matters of military innovation and planning.

The video below is the 3rd most frequently viewed video on TEDTV.com with over 45 million views as of August, 2019.

Simon Sinek: *"How Great Leaders Inspire Action"* http://www. ted.com/talks/simon_sinek_how_great_leaders_inspire_action. html?source=email#.T5Wc3b4ulWh.email

Simon Sinek describes *"How Great Leaders Inspire Action,"* in terms of the Golden Circle as the following illustration depicts. It is a simple concept, but very powerful. For one, if we answer the why, as we discussed in the section on communication, we are answering the very reason for initiating action in the first place. If you, as a leader can speak to people at this level, and get them to believe in "why" they do what they do, the "how" and the "what" just happen. It is when a person doesn't have a firm grasp as to "why" they do something that they lack the proper motivation to do it. If that motivation comes from within, or is intrinsic in nature, the likelihood of success will be greater because they are doing it for themselves, not for someone else.

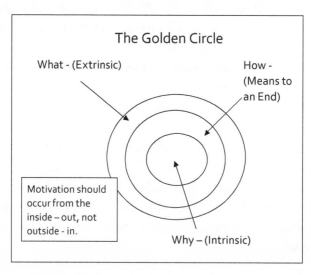

As an example, if a construction company wanted to sit down and hash out the "why", "how" and "what" of their work, it may look something like this.

Why we do what we do
We believe in making the ideas, and dreams of our clients come true.
How we do what we do
We treat every person and project as our primary concern.
What we do
We build.

Often we tell people "what" they need to do and "how" they need to do it, but we forget to explain "why" they need to do it. Take for example medicine, we understand "what" needs to be done - take care of patients, and we understand "how" to take care of patients, (learned this in school) but the gap often comes when we can't agree on "why" we take care of patients. Some nurses are called to medicine because they want to take care of people and they find personal satisfaction in making the lives of others better or less painful. The act of caring for others is all the motivation they need and they derive satisfaction and need fulfillment from the act itself. The "how" and "what" are secondary. The desire to be in medicine is from an intrinsic place of motivation.

On the other hand, there are practitioners that find their motivation from extrinsic sources, such as money, prestige, or a favorable schedule. They go to school and learn "what" it is and "how" to be a provide care through orientation, and then the "why" of being a care giver is lost or misaligned with other care givers that desire intrinsic motivation. This incongruous motivation causes problems. The belief systems that these two groups operate under are at opposite ends of the spectrum.

"If you hire people just because they can do a
job, they'll work for your money.
But if you hire people who believe what you believe,
they'll work for you with blood and sweat and tears." (Simon Sinek)

The key to developing a team that is motivated by the proper "why," is to hire people who are motivated intrinsically. Hire people who find their reward in bringing client's dreams to reality, not for money, not for working hours and not for prestige.

*Motivation should flow from the inside (intrinsically)
to the outside (extrinsically), not the opposite.*

2. **Classical Theory of Motivation** – Money is the sole motivator for workers. Fredrick Taylor believed that productivity was related to financial incentive. He suggested that workers who were paid more would produce more. Time and time again, and study after study has proven this theory inaccurate.

Money isn't the most powerful motivator.

3. **Hawthorne Studies** – in 1924, Elton Mayo and his colleagues from Harvard University tried to link physical conditions to productivity. They wanted to look at things such as light and noise levels in the work environment. What they discovered was no matter what the physical changes to the environment were, productivity increased. This was not the expected result. What they discovered through interviews with the employees involved in the study was that the employees expressed satisfaction not only because their co-workers were friendly, but because their supervisors had asked for their help and input in the study. To state this in simpler terms, the researchers found that employees were not responding to the change in physical conditions, they were responding positively to the attention they received from management and researchers. Elton Mayo and his colleagues concluded that social and psychological factors could significantly affect productivity, satisfaction and morale.

   The Hawthorne studies opened the door to the idea that human relations influence employees and productivity. It was concluded that managers who attend to the needs, beliefs, and expectations of their people, will have more success when trying to motivate employees.

Taking an interest and showing we care is a powerful motivator.

4. **Maslow's Needs Hierarchy of Motivation** – This theory illustrates the five basic needs people have and the order in which they strive to reach them. We cannot skip over a lower level need to a higher level need without obtaining them in sequential order. Satisfaction must

be obtained in the lower level need before we can move to a higher level need. Our interest is in understanding how leaders align work with the attainment of higher order needs.

A person who is cold and starving is not going to worry about respect from his or her colleagues until he or she is warm and hunger is satiated.

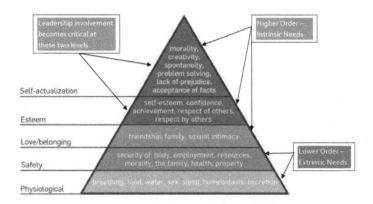

1st Level Needs – Physiological Needs (Extrinsic) – Obtaining employment will provide shelter and food. It will also make the potential for sex more likely, but of course that will still need to be handled outside of work.

2nd Level Needs – Safety and Security (Extrinsic) – Employment will provide a means to maintaining food and shelter on an on-going basis, and the result is the safety need is satisfied.

3rd Level Needs – Social (Intrinsic) – Employment will provide a venue to develop social relationships, teams, and acceptance from others. This is the first stage in attaining higher order needs that come from intrinsic motivation rather than extrinsic motivation.

4th Level Needs – Self-Esteem (Intrinsic) – This is where leadership gets involved and can really make employment a worthwhile venture for both the employee and the organization. Self-esteem can be obtained through the development of mutually respectful and valuable relationships. An organization should not hire an employee unless the organization can truly value and respect the employee's contributions. Leaders can get more from employees if they can recognize the employee's contributions and acknowledge them in a meaningful way. By doing so, the manager is assisting the employee with one of the higher order needs and producing a higher functioning person who feels good about themselves and their work.

5th Level Needs – Self –Actualization (Intrinsic) – Concerning employment, if leaders encourage employees and assist them in obtaining this need, the sky is the limit. We want employees to open their wings and soar. This is the most dynamic aspect of the employment relationship. Once the employee has attained the lower order needs, they will desire to maximize their full-potential. This is also the place where a leader can reap the most reward as well. A leader's goal should be to help each employee be the best they can be. Of course, this will require effort and interest from the employee and encouragement and commitment from the leader, and the organization. The concept is simple, if a leader can keep as many employees as possible striving for self-actualization, reaching it, and moving on to the next challenge, it becomes a win/win for both the employee and organization. The organization will have a long-term engaged employee and the employee will constantly strive to become self-actualized while fulfilling intrinsic needs.

5. **Douglas McGregor's Theory X – (The Negative)** McGregor sorted through all the different management approaches, ideas and viewpoints and distilled them down to a very common derivative – positive and negative approaches.
Theory X managers believe that:

A. Employees do not want to work
B. Employees dislike work and will try to avoid work
C. Employees need to be coerced to work, must be strictly controlled and threatened to achieve organizational goals.

D. Employees prefer to be directed and do not like to make decisions. They avoid responsibility and have little ambition for achievement.

This style of management (it is management – no leadership happening here) lends itself to a culture of fear and intimidation, micro-management, and very little creativity and innovation. These managers often think no one can do the job as well as they could, so they prescribe very tight controls over their employees. They ask for little or no input from their employees and make decisions in an autocratic style as discussed in the last chapter. This type of manager does not consider that employees may be able to obtain social, self-esteem and self-actualization needs through work, because they believe employees are only working as a means to food, shelter, and security.

6. **Douglas McGregor's Theory Y – (The Positive)** This approach is a more humanistic approach toward work. Leaders who subscribe to this style believe people want to do a good job, and that they will strive to attain social, esteem and even self-actualization needs if given the proper environment and conditions.

McGregor describes the assumptions behind Theory Y in the following way:

A. The expenditure of physical and mental effort in work is as natural as play or rest.
B. People will exercise self-direction and self-control to achieve objectives to which they are committed.
C. People will commit to objectives when they realize that the achievement of those goals will bring them internal, personal reward.
D. The average person will seek and accept responsibility.
E. Imagination, ingenuity and creativity can help solve organizational problems.
F. Organizations today do not make full use of worker's intellectual potential.

Theory X and Y are the self-fulfilling prophecy in action. If you believe an employee is good or bad, motivated or unmotivated, they'll often respond to exactly the way we treat them.

7. Equity Theory

Equity theory describes that how much a person is willing to give an organization is dependent on the reward they will receive for their efforts.

If for example, we believe that our efforts or the amount of work we are asked to perform are more valuable to the organization than the reward we receive, we will only perform the amount of work we feel is equal to the reward we will receive. People compare their input in skill, experience, and effort and assess how that compares to the output, or reward of other people. If they feel their input and output is similar to that of others, or in proportion they feel there is equity. If there isn't equity, they work to create equity by asking to increase their output, in the form of pay, or by decreasing their peers output by trying to have co-workers paid less or by just doing less to balance the scales of justice. If there is inequity in an employee's perception of the input and output, they will most likely look for another job that can provide a sense of equity. This can manifest itself intrinsically and extrinsically.

What we get from an employer, must equal what we feel we should earn. If it is perceived to be out of balance, people will actively work to balance it. We may slack off, steal, sabotage our supervisors or speak negatively about the company, supervisor or co-workers to attain equity.

Balance can also be attained through appreciation, recognition, respect, trust, honesty and fair treatment. It is not strictly related to compensation.

8. Expectancy Theory

States that the more likely we are to obtain a certain reward, the more motivated we will be to obtain it. If the likelihood of obtaining a reward is scarce, then the motivation will not be strong.

People won't even try to attain an unrealistic goal and in fact,
may sabotage it to prove just how unrealistic it is.

9. **Two-Factor Theory of Motivation** – (also referred to as Motivation-Hygiene Theory) Frederick Herzberg developed this theory of motivation. It distinguishes between two factors, hygiene and motivators.

    1. **Hygiene factors** – **(Extrinsic)** - involves the presence or absence of job dissatisfiers, including working conditions, pay, company policies and interpersonal relationships. (Daft, Marcic, 415)

        If these factors are absent, employees feel dissatisfied with their work, however if they are present, the dissatisfaction is removed, but they do not become highly satisfied, or motivated to excel. These are the extrinsic motivators, and they only remove dissatisfaction, they do not create satisfaction. These are similar to the lower order needs in Maslow's Needs Hierarchy – physiological, safety and social needs.

    2. **Motivation factors** – **(Intrinsic)** - influence job satisfaction based on fulfillment of high-level needs such as achievement, recognition, responsibility and opportunity for growth. (Daft, Marcic, 415)

        When these factors are not present, we feel neutral toward work, but if they are present, we feel motivated to perform at higher levels and become satisfied. These are the intrinsic motivators, and if they are fulfilled, we will likely be satisfied. They are similar to the higher order needs that Maslow described; social, self-esteem, and self-actualization.

For the hygiene theory to actually motivate employees and make them fully satisfied, it requires the two parts of the system operate in conjunction for success. If one is present and the other isn't, the outcome is the same, a neutral feeling toward work. For the Two Factor Theory to be successful both hygiene factors and motivational factors must be present.

As this relates to Maslow's Needs Hierarchy, if employees are struggling to find the right equipment because there isn't enough, and they are stretched too thin personnel wise, they effectively are huddled in a corner freezing and starving. They are trying to obtain the basic needs of food, shelter, water and safety. Yet, so often we ask them to be social, engage the client, smile and improve self-esteem and ultimately be all they can be and find self-actualization. Simply put, if the hygiene factors are not present there is no reason to even talk about motivators, or higher order needs. They are just trying to survive. This is why client satisfaction suffers, yet we too often do not want to admit that we have set everyone up for misery and a day spent treading water. The need or desire for more, more, more and more growth from industry is a principle concern when it comes to the well-being of our future workers. Growth is not infinite and at some point too much growth and diminishing resources means we have to eat ourselves.

Hygiene-Motivation Theory

While working at a hospital, the Motivation – Hygiene Theory became a reality and illustrated to me exactly how it worked in real time. Hospitals are reimbursed by the Centers for Medicare/Medicaid Services (CMS) at varying percentages based on patient satisfaction survey scores. Therefore, it is important to hospitals to drive up these patient satisfaction scores so that revenue climbs as well.

There was a huge push around 2010 to increase these scores. A campaign was launched to ensure employees and their treatment of patients pushed those scores along with reimbursement upward. As I interacted with the nurses and physicians about the plans, goals and expectations to ensure we maximized revenue and patient satisfaction, they very adamantly informed me that this would be difficult. One nurse asked, "How are we supposed to make the patient's 'very satisfied,' when it takes us 45 minutes to find a blood pressure cuff?" Another said, "There aren't enough thermometers, either." They were right. I confirmed with the Unit Directors that this was an on-going issue.

How can the hospital, or anyone ask healthcare practitioners to provide excellent care and make the patients feel good about it when they are spending their time running around being non-productive, making the patient wait, in a time-crunch and becoming increasingly frustrated.

The hygiene factors, (the basic working conditions) were far below satisfactory for the care providers. It was unrealistic to ask them to provide excellent, satisfying care and for them to feel good and satisfied about their own jobs when the basic tools necessary to perform their jobs were not adequate – blood pressure cuffs and thermometers.

What we realized was that little pockets of nurses were hoarding the equipment for their small group's usage and not making the equipment available to the greater group. Of course, they did this because they saw an opportunity to ensure their work days would go smooth in spite of everyone else. They knew these items were a hot commodity.

We found the funds and were able to purchase new equipment so our people could do their jobs, and at least feel neutral about their work, rather, than dissatisfied. It would be no different on a construction site, if a carpenter had to wait ten minutes to make one cut. It would be like waiting in line to use a saw, or sharing a hammer. The product would suffer, employee and client satisfaction would suffer and schedules would never be met.

You can't expect an outstanding product and satisfied clients if people don't have the basic necessities to perform their work. It's like giving the best racecar driver in the world a stock, Hyundai Elantra and asking him to win the Indianapolis 500. It simply won't happen.

10. **Reinforcement Perspective of Motivation** advocates the appropriate use of rewards and punishments to modify behaviors. The goal of reinforcement theory is to encourage or deter certain behaviors. Behavior modification is the goal and this is carried out on the assumption that behavior that is positively reinforced will be repeated and behavior that is not reinforced will not be repeated.

   There are four reinforcement tools available to change human behavior:

   A. **Positive Reinforcement** – to actively give pleasant and positive feedback for desired behavior whether in verbal, financial, or other forms. For example, when we see someone doing what they should, tell them, "Good job," and explain why it's a good job. This will encourage the behavior to continue. Ambiguity is always the enemy.

B. **Avoidance Learning** – is producing a desired outcome so negative consequences will cease. For example, if an employee stops a certain behavior, the supervisor will stop nagging them about it.

C. **Punishment** – is to subject unpleasant consequences on someone for undesired behavior. This is not exactly a favorable way to motivate people, due to the fact it fails to explain the correct way to behave, and is often demeaning. It could also create fear and intimidation.

D. **Extinction** – if a behavior is not rewarded the behavior will cease to exist or become extinct. For example, if an employee fails to receive raises because they are short and nasty to co-workers, they may stop being short and nasty in order to have the reward of increases reinstated.

Reinforcement Perspective of Motivation

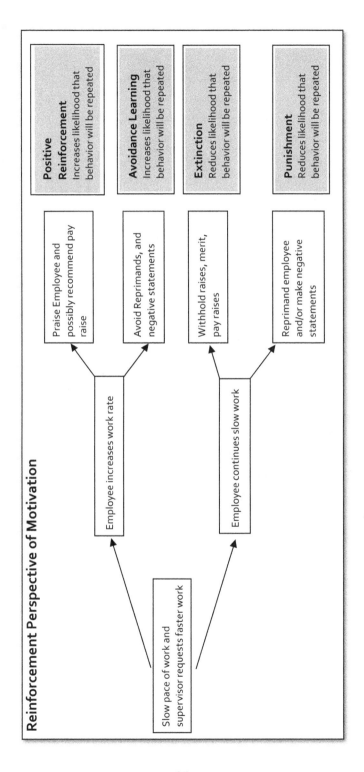

Slow pace of work and supervisor requests faster work

Employee increases work rate

Employee continues slow work

Praise Employee and possibly recommend pay raise

Avoid Reprimands, and negative statements

Withhold raises, merit, pay raises

Reprimand employee and/or make negative statements

Positive Reinforcement
Increases likelihood that behavior will be repeated

Avoidance Learning
Increases likelihood that behavior will be repeated

Extinction
Reduces likelihood that behavior will be repeated

Punishment
Reduces likelihood that behavior will be repeated

Motivation

It was half time of a basketball game toward the end of my senior year in high school. I averaged 22 points per game and had already signed an letter of intent for a full scholarship to play at a small NAIA college. At halftime I had 4 points. We were losing which we didn't do often. The head coach had played basketball at a small college as well. He came into the locker room. His body shook. He looked around wildly and then caught my eye. He stared at me like I intentionally missed shots. He snapped back into a crazed frenzy and threw a water bottle just above my head. Water spewed everywhere. I was already soaked in sweat so it didn't matter, but it pissed me off.

The team and assistant coach sat quiet and watched his tirade. He turned in circles and looked for something to take his aggression out on. He chose the pile of shooting jerseys on the floor. He kicked them. From the pile a jersey opened up on the wall – 34. Serendipitously, it was mine. He went on for the reminder of the halftime berating me for taking a bad shot and missing others. He threatened to put me on the bench. I was cold. Even Larry Bird had cold streaks. He spat when he yelled and spittle gathered in the corners of his mouth.

He lost the team after the jersey incident, but we sat quietly and pretended to listen anyway. My team and I dragged our *sses off the bench in the locker room and filed back onto the court. The assistant coach gave me a nod, squinted and waved me to step to the side. He had also played basketball in college. He was All-SEC 1st Team and selected in the 10th round of the NBA draft from Vanderbilt University. His claim to fame was that he held Pistol Pete Maravich below his scoring average. I asked, "What was his average?" My coach said, "43 a game." I asked, "What'd he score on you?" "42," he said and raised his eyebrows as if to say, "how about that!?"

I stepped to the side and let the rest of the team go ahead. He put his arm around me and we walked slowly, together. He said, "Don't listen to him. If you don't shoot the ball 20 times this half you're letting this team down. You're one of the best shooters I've ever seen. It'll change." Sure enough, it did. I didn't shoot twenty times, but scored 22 points and we won.

The point is this. I was the type of player and person that wasn't going to be motivated through external forces like fear, punishment or accolades. The only thing that yelling at me and ranting and raving was going to do, was make me want to fight you, certainly not play for you. I wasn't playing for him anyway. I was playing because I loved basketball and I loved my team. One coach new this and the other didn't. One was a leader and the other a manager. One used positive reinforcement and the other tried to use punishment.

*It is through the **Law of Effect** that these principles come to light. The Law of Effect states that positive reinforcement encourages continued, desirable behavior, and negatively reinforced behavior inhibits the continuation of undesirable behavior. In the instance above, I would have had to have been trying to miss shots for his approach to have even had a chance of working.*

It is a more desirable approach to positively reinforce behavior rather than to negatively reinforce behavior. Learning organizations want employees to grow and feel good about their work, not fear the outcomes of poor work. Again, it is the difference between developing a culture of fear and intimidation, and one of mutual respect and growth.

It is the way a leader uses communication, encourages and motivates people in the Infinite Space between Management and Skill Set that drives behavior.

"Fear creates anger, anger creates hatred and hatred creates suffering." (Yoda the Master Jedi)

11. **Empowerment** – is a process of sharing power with employees, thereby enhancing confidence in their ability to perform their jobs and their belief that they are influential contributors to the organization. (Bateman, Snell, 425)

    It is a very powerful way to illustrate to an employee that they are valuable, capable, and qualified to do the job they have been hired for. It is also a powerful way to get people to buy-in to goal attainment. Often though, manager's say, "You are empowered to do what needs done," and then when the employee does what they think to be right, they get an ear full from the manager who says, "That's not what I would have done." Managers cannot send mixed messages. They can set parameters, but they cannot undermine decisions. This will make people stagnant and unmotivated. Saying, "I empower you," is a joke. To actually empower someone, the leader needs to make the environment conducive to a real diffusion of power, and put it into the hands of the people who can affect change.

Fostering Empowerment is a process not a grandiose declaration. It happens through action no so much words.

The following factors are necessary to create an environment of empowerment where everyone feels they have a real influence over performance standards and business effectiveness within their area of responsibility. To do so, these factors must be present. (Bateman, Snell, 426)

Empowerment isn't a grandiose declaration, it is what happens in the Infinite Space between the declaration and the outcomes that inspiration and leadership resides.

Tips for Fostering Empowerment

1. **Information** – information must flow freely and must be relevant to the success of the employee.
2. **Knowledge** – employees need to know how to use the information which means they must be adequately oriented and trained to make decisions based on the information and the resources available.
3. **Power** – must be given adequately so that employees can take the information they are given, the knowledge they have gained and make decisions that give them proper control over their work to succeed.
4. **Rewards** – upon success, rewards must be given to the employee. The rewards that come from empowerment are often *intrinsic* in nature and come in the form of a sense of accomplishment,

control, ownership and buy-in to their work-life. To close the loop of empowerment secondary rewards or *extrinsic* rewards such as a thank you note, pat on the back, public recognition or even a small token of appreciation are useful tools.

If a leader isn't confident in the people they've hired, and can't relinquish power to the people they've put in place to make things work, it usually isn't the employee's fault.

Empowerment

My wife, Amy and I moved to Denver shortly after we were married. I worked at an outpatient imaging center as the Human Resources Manager. We did PET scans, Nuc Med, MRI, CT, X-ray, US, etc. There was a bonus plan in place and each month it paid $100-200 dollars. It was based on the number of scans we were able to do each month. The center owners pushed for growth. Space was limited and we'd already expanded to the third floor and bottom level. By all accounts the modality leaders could not fit any more patients into the available time slots. I didn't buy it.

I spent a few days and walked around, sat with and talked to the modality leaders. I asked them how their schedules worked. I asked them to walk me through a scan and show me what the important pieces of their jobs were. Every single one of them jumped at the chance to share their work with me. Remember, everyone wants to be an expert. Think of the Hawthorn Effect as well, just asking someone's input is powerful. I asked questions which they eagerly answered.

I told them I was asked how we could improve the number of scans per day. I also told them that this was going to provide the framework for a new bonus plan. I calculated the number of scans we would need to do in each modality to meet the financial goals of the imaging center. I developed a bonus structure that would pay $500.00/month if we could reach those numbers. The next point is critical. I asked them all to come to a meeting. It was just the modality leads and me. I showed them all what each groups necessary numbers were and said if we can brainstorm a way to reach these numbers there's another $300-400/month in it for everyone.

I explained that if we could figure out a way to schedule their people *and improve the efficiency of their exams, we all would reap the rewards. We met again a week later. Each of the leaders had gone from, "there isn't enough room for more patients," to a bona fide plan to reach the increased number of exams. In some cases, like PET, it was on average one additional exam per day, but in other areas, like X-ray, it was ten additional cases per day, all without increasing overtime. The center went from $800,000 in revenue per month to $1.3 million over the course of the next year and we added 25 people, and MRI, CT and Ultrasound units.*

*Everyone in the entire place received a monthly bonus of $500.00 which eventually grew to upwards of $700.00. How did this happen? We linked the success of each modality to their own needs. People felt like they were getting what they were giving – the **equity** theory at work. People felt like the likelihood of obtaining a reward was good because they had control of obtaining it – the **expectancy** theory at work. Finally, they were **empowered** to figure out their own plan for obtaining the goals. It wasn't someone else's plan to redesign the workday, schedule or flow of patients. It was theirs and they owned it. They were empowered. They bought in and sold it to their employees.*

"If employees plan the fight, they won't fight the plan." DD Eisenhower

What's Your Motive?

As a leader, you should be open to the idea that different people see the world differently. We discussed in the chapter on Diversity and the Changing Management Paradigm, the idea that different generations have different ideas related to work, which also means they are motivated by different drivers. For example, Generation X wants empowerment, innovation, participation, and teamwork. Generation Y values technology, family, they are confident, crave feedback and want to achieve and be recognized.

Which leadership style is effective varies with the people being managed and led. To motivate people, Martin Maeher and Larry Braskamp advise managers to assess their people's motives and adjust their or leadership style accordingly – the (**Contingency Theory of Leadership**.) Challenge employees who value accomplishment to try new things and to exhibit excellence. Give those who value recognition the attention they crave. Place those who value affiliation on a team that has a family feeling and that shares in decision making. Motivate those who value power with competition and opportunities for triumphant success. Different strokes for different folks, but for each a way to energize and direct – in a word, to motivate – behavior. (Myers, 376)

The idea of motivation comes in different forms for different people. A leader's role is to determine what needs an employee desires to have filled and work with them to fulfill those needs (refer to **Maslow**). The act of concern alone (the **Hawthorne Effect**) will provide positive results. The identification of employee motivators (**intrinsic or extrinsic**) will steer us to provide what the employee lacks. The understanding as to how an employee thinks will allow the leader to provide **equity** and meet **expectations** of goal attainment.

As a leader, ensure the **Hygiene** factors are not draining your employees and are at a minimum keeping them primed for increased motivation and satisfaction. This means equipment, resources and the environment need to be satisfactory at least. Then guide employees and help them reach their self-esteem goals, and ultimately find self-actualization, (refer to **Herzberg's Two-Factory Theory/Maslow Needs Hierarchy.**)

This can seem like a daunting task, but the investment at the front-end will pay huge dividends at the back-end. Employees will be autonomous, energized and have a positive attitude toward work. Leaders will not have to deal with trite employee grievances, disputes, and misguided negativity. Ultimately, a mutual respect will be attained and the employee and leader will look out for one another and strive to see the other succeed, and know that one cannot succeed without the other's success. We will have developed teams that push in the same direction, no matter how steep the hill, toward the same objective and after the same goals; (refer to **Goal-Setting Theory.**)

Leaders must let their ego, go.
Realize that the success and sense of accomplishment and
control an employee feels is the best gift we can give them.
Leaders motivate by making other's better.

CHAPTER 5

ORGANIZATIONAL DEVELOPMENT, CHANGE AND INNOVATION

Overview on Organizational Development, Change and Innovation

As we progresses through work and life, one thing is absolutely certain, change. Change is like gravity. We know that items fall to earth at the rate of 9.8 meters per second squared. Just as we trust we will stick to earth, we should also trust that each day, change of some sort will occur. Once we've agreed to this idea, and once we've come to terms with the constant and given nature of change we can embrace it, rather than dread it as if it is some looming and unfortunate surprise.

Just like we naturally embrace the fact that gravity will always be there, pushing us back to earth, we can embrace the idea that change will always be there pushing us as well. If so, we have a better likelihood of harnessing the inevitable power of change and directing it toward better outcomes.

Change, just like gravity, is constant and will always occur.

Change is Constant

Imagine if a professional baseball pitcher constantly wondered if when he threw a pitch, gravity would push the ball to earth or whether gravity would cease to exist and the ball would streak into the ether of outer space. The uncertainty of this would cause him to alter his pitch, and leave him wondering if in fact gravity would be there to help him or hurt him.

Because of the constant nature of gravity, he trusts that it will be there, consistently working on each pitch, every time. The key is that he doesn't question whether or not gravity will affect his pitch; he knows it and uses that force to throw strikes. He understands that gravity is a constant and he embraces it. Change is a constant and we can either embrace it or wither.

If we agree that change is inevitable and constant, we can use it to benefit the people around us, and ourselves as leaders, just like a major league pitcher uses gravity to help him throw strikes. Change is often thought of as a negative, because people sometimes cannot concede to the fact that change happens whether we like it, fight it or embrace it. Some people like to fight change. Others embrace it and view it as a positive opportunity to learn something and develop a new perspective on an issue or experience.

Some people pretend that change is not happening around them, all the time. People want to act like change isn't occurring if they don't acknowledge it. One could argue that change is uncertain and for some, uncertainty is scary, and as we learned in the last chapter, "Fear creates anger, anger creates hatred and hatred creates suffering." When in fact, change isn't uncertain at all. It happens all the time and always will. The only thing uncertain about change is how it will manifest. What form will change take?

If we can accept the idea that change isn't something to fear; but that change is something we can dictate, control and manipulate, it becomes our friend, and opens the door for improvement, increased satisfaction, and innovation. In fact, all the luxuries and niceties in life are a result of change and more importantly, innovation. If we as leaders can embrace the consistency of change, and encourage our co-workers to accept this, and expect it, the barriers to change, improvement and innovation will lessen.

One can change a process and make things different, or create a completely new and original idea (innovation) that will solve a problem. **Change management** is an approach to shifting/transitioning individuals, teams and organizations from a current state to a desired future state. It is an organizational process aimed at helping stakeholders accept and embrace changes in their business environment.

General Reasons for Resistance to Change

Even if we, as leaders, grow to understand that change is inevitable, and something that we can embrace, we still have to understand the obstacles people may have with the change process. Of course understanding what obstacles may be present is the first step in being able to overcome those obstacles. A leader can scan the environment to try to identify which of these obstacles may be present in order to prioritize which may be interfering with the change initiative.

1. **Inertia** – Often, people do not want to disturb the status quo. The old ways of doing things are comfortable and easy, so people don't want to shake things up and try something new. But remember as Lew Platt, the former CEO of Hewlett Packard said,

"What made you successful in the past, won't in the future."

2. **Timing** – People often resist change because of poor timing. If we are unusually busy or under stress, or if relations between leaders and workers are strained, the timing is wrong for introducing new proposals. Where possible, leaders should introduce change when people are receptive.
3. **Surprise** – One key aspect of timing and receptivity is surprise. If the change is sudden, unexpected, or extreme, resistance may be the initial, almost reflexive reaction. One must have time to prepare for the change.
4. **Peer pressure** – Sometimes work teams resist new ideas. Even if individual members do not strongly oppose a change suggested by leadership, the team may band together in opposition. (Bateman Snell, 584)

Just as change is a given, so is the resistance to change. The critical factor is how change is introduced and what skills we have as leaders to overcome resistance and settle on change that is agreeable to the most people. When administering a change, the Utilitarian Approach is advised. What's going to provide the greatest good for the greatest number of people? Just as we've discussed in prior chapters, there are positive and negative approaches to everything. We can choose to take an approach that mirrors the ideas and beliefs of a Theory Y leader or we can choose an approach that mimics that of the authoritarian, Theory X manager. A Theory X approach would yield quick change at the front-end, but major issues at the tail-end. Whereas, a Theory Y approach will take time at the beginning of change, but have better, more stable results at the tail-end.

We need to till the ground of change, fertilize it, plant
the seed, water it, pick the weeds and then let the change
take root and harvest the fruits of our labor. It is what
happens in the Space between planting the seed and
harvesting the crop that will determine success.

Methods for Dealing with Resistance to Change

Approach	Commonly used in situations	Advantages	Drawbacks
Education and Communication (Positive)	Where there is a lack of information or inaccurate information and analysis. are involved.	Once persuaded, people will often help with the implementation of the change.	Can be very time-consuming
Participation and Involvement (Positive)	Where the initiators do not have all the information they need to design the change, and where others have considerable power to resist.	People who participate will be committed to implementing change, and any relevant information they have will be integrated into the change plan.	Can be time-consuming if participators design an inappropriate change.
Facilitation and Support (Positive)	Where people are resisting because of adjustment problems.	No other approach works as well with adjustment problems.	Can be time-consuming and expensive, and still fail.
Negotiation and Agreement (Neutral)	Where someone or some group will clearly lose out in a change, and where that group has considerable power to resist.	Sometimes it is a relatively easy way to avoid major resistance.	Can be too expensive in many cases if it alerts others to negotiate.
Manipulation and Cooptation (Negative)	Where other tactics will not work, or are too expensive.	It can be a relatively quick and inexpensive solution to resistance problems.	Can lead to future problems if people feel manipulated.
Explicit and Implicit (Negative)	Where speed is essential, and the change initiators possess considerable power.	It is speedy and can overcome any kind of resistance.	Can be risky if it leaves people angry at initiators.

Planned Change Models

Kurt Lewin introduced a Change Theory in the 1940's that was built around *unfreezing* behavior, *moving* behavior and *refreezing* behavior. These three ideas were expanded on by Edgar Schein by applying psychological understanding to each stage. To further understand how the three stage model fits into the idea of Organizational Development we must understand this concept. **Organizational Development** is planned change. As we know, change is constant and presents something new and different to us. With organizational development, leaders first need to identify what needs changed, and then how. Once that has been established we can apply the Three Stage Model for Change.

For change to occur a current process, procedure, style or format must become weak or less useful, or have the potential to become weak or less useful. The spark for change is a gap. Change is the result of something faltering or not meeting the expected needs. A **gap** exists between what is needed and what is being received. **Change** is the process of becoming different. Ideally, we want to focus on **proactive** change rather than **reactive** change. This will be addressed on the following pages.

"Necessity is the mother of invention." (Plato)
Interpretation
Difficult situations inspire ingenious solutions.

Time invested at the front-end of a change process is much better spent than at the tail-end of the process fixing what could have been avoided if time and attention were given at the beginning.

It is the investment up front in...

1. **Employee Input**
2. **Employee Buy-in**
3. **Employee communication about fears, apprehensions, and ideas...**

   ...that will reap the most positive and effective results to the change process.

So often leaders identify a problem like poor client satisfaction and throw a half-cocked gimmick at it and walk away. Leaders do not involve the people who will be responsible for the day-to-day process change to identify obstacles or shortcomings. Often it is because leaders juggle multiple change initiatives and then when they have too many initiatives in the air and become overwhelmed they delegate one or more initiatives to someone else and tell them to implement them.

The most alarming part of this strategy is that the leader comes back a month later and expects the change to have taken hold. If it didn't, the leader scrambles to put together another solution and then throws it at the problem again. The worst part is we call this progress, just so we can say we did something, or worse, we look for other reasons why the "change" didn't take root, and assign blame. The answer is; we didn't nurture it or water it. We just threw what may have been a viable solution or seed at a dried up field and hoped for the best. We need to prepare the environment and people for change at the front-end.

Invest your effort, energy and time at the front-end of the change process and as change occurs, it will get easier.

Invest Time, Energy and Attention at the Front-End of Change

It is similar to the idea of a family moving, and taking a child out of one school and putting them in a new school. You can simply move, have the child wait at the bus stop the first day of school and hope they figure it out in a reasonable amount of time without much anguish. Most likely however, they will run into obstacles, unfamiliar situations, and won't know their way around.

*Or... you can tell the child that you may be moving to give them time to prepare mentally for the change. This lets them deal with the potential and allows them to **Unfreeze** their current paradigms. Then when the decision is made, explain to them why it was made and that they will be attending a really great school. Go to Google earth – do a fly over. Browse the school's website. Let them get familiar. Tell the child the reasons why the new school will be better and then take them to it so they can have the mental image of the school in their head and start imagining themselves* *there. Take them on a tour of the school and arrange for them to meet their teacher in advance. You could even let them shadow a selected student for a day and get to know the way things work and maybe meet a few kids that will be in his/her new class.*

*That investment of time and information at the front-end may positively transition your child from his/her old school to his/her new school and make the situation better because he or she can leave behind the bad stuff. This allows them to shift or **Move** their paradigm about school. Because you've focused your attention on the front-end of the change, the back end will be smoother.*

*Eventually, they will settle in and the new paradigm of what school is will **Refreeze** into their current reality. Or....you can throw the child in the new school without communicating or investing any time, energy, or effort at the front-end and have a disgruntled, disobedient child who acts out and needs thousands of dollars of therapy. It is your call. You are the leader. You are in charge.*

It's no different at work. People are people no matter what age. In fact, adults adjust to change less readily than children. Children are made of clay and rubber and adults are harden into fired pots, and concrete.

Lewin's Three Stage Model for Planned Change

This model describes the cognitive gymnastics people bound through to get to the other side of change. Remember, change starts at point A and ends at point B. The quickest way from one point to another is a straight line. The key is to take time to work through with tact, not a bulldozer, the cognitive obstacles that people will inevitably throw in the path of change. Change very rarely ever looks like a straight line. The goal is to minimize the deviations from the path of change.

Stage 1 – Unfreezing (Allowing oneself to consider change)

The disconfirmation of a process creates pain and discomfort, which cause guilt and anxiety, which motivates the person to change. But unless the person feels comfortable with dropping the old behaviors and acquiring new ones, change will not occur. That is, the person must experience a sense of psychological safety in order to replace the old behaviors with new behaviors. *(Like explaining to your child they will be attending a new school, showing them the new school and touring the new school. Of course, they need to understand the "why" for change.)*

Stage 2 – Moving (The person shifts their cognitive paradigm to begin change)

The person undergoes cognitive restructuring. The person needs information and evidence to show that the change is desirable, possible and positive. This is gained by modeling the behavior of an exemplar or by gathering relevant information from the environment. *(Like explaining the benefits of the new school to your child, he/she gaining new friends, and enjoying their new teacher.)*

Stage 3 – Refreezing (The idea that the change is good. It takes hold and change becomes real.)

Integrate the new behaviors into the person's personality and attitudes. That is, stabilizing the change requires testing to see if they fit – fit with the individual, and fit with the individual's social surroundings. Significant relationships are important people in the person's social environment – do these significant others accept and approve of the changes? (French, Bell, 82) *(The child embracing the new school and talk of the old school stopping.)*

Investments in Change – Each Zig of the Arrow, is an Obstacle

<u>Front–end</u> - **Change Line from Point A to Point B** - obstacles and paradigms are overcome at the beginning as illustrated by the slowly straightening arrows that represent the ***assimilation of change.***

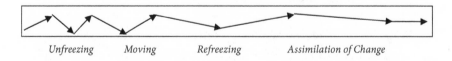

Unfreezing   Moving   Refreezing   Assimilation of Change

<u>Back-end</u> - **Change Line from Point A to Point B** – this change line illustrates that a change has been neglected at the front end and problems occurred at the tail-end which lead to the ***extinction of change.***

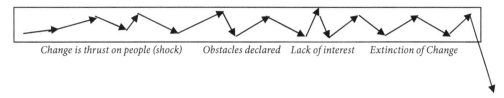

Change is thrust on people (shock)　　*Obstacles declared*　*Lack of interest*　　*Extinction of Change*

Participation and Empowerment for Planned Change

Empowerment is not only relevant in our discussions about leadership but it is equally important to discuss empowerment when talking about change and innovation.

Refer to the Chapter on Motivation for a refresher on tips for empowerment. The excerpt below is a synopsis from research that links the importance of empowerment to involvement, participation, acceptance of decisions, increased commitment, lower stress levels, better solutions to problems and energized performance.

"One of the most important foundations of Organization Development (OD) is its use of the participation/empowerment model. Participation in OD programs is not restricted to elites or the top people; it is extended broadly throughout the organization. Increased participation and empowerment have always been central goals and prominent values of the field. These pillars of OD practice are validated by both research and practice. Research on group dynamics began in the 1940's and achieved exponential growth in the 1950s and 1960s. This research demonstrated that increased involvement and participation were desired by most people, had the ability to energize greater performance, produce better solutions to problems, and greatly enhanced acceptance of decisions. It was found that such group dynamics worked to overcome resistance to change, increased commitment to the organization, reduced stress levels, and generally made people feel better about themselves and their worlds. Participation is a powerful elixir – it is good for people, and it dramatically improves individual and organizational performance. To empower is to give someone power. This is done by giving individuals the authority to participate, to make decisions, to contribute their ideas, to exert influence, and to be responsible. This is why participation is such an effective form of empowerment. Participation enhances empowerment, and empowerment in turn enhances performance and individual well-being." (French, Bell, 94)

Creating a Participative, Empowered and Innovative Culture

Innovation is a more specialized kind of change, it is a new idea applied to initiating or improving a product, process or service, (Robbins, 571)

For innovation to occur, an environment of creativity, security, acceptance of failure, empowerment and adequate resources must be available. We will look at how to embrace innovation as a leader and as an organization.

Even crazy ideas may spark brilliance.

Have you ever been sitting around talking with friends, and someone says something ridiculous, but because of some little aspect of their ridiculous comment, your brain goes into a new direction, down the path to brilliance? Would your idea ever have come to fruition, if it weren't for the person coming out of left field in a seemingly unrelated way? It's hard to tell, but often what crazy, off-the-wall ideas do is cut through a lot of mundane thought that can get mired in old paradigms.

Crazy ideas are often out of our comfort zone. Therefore, as we know, we have a tendency to negate or marginalize ideas and people that aren't like us. The key to embracing and creating a climate that is participative, empowered and innovative is to be open-minded, encourage the absurd, weird and even ideas that seem nonsensical. It may just take you down the path to a solution. You never know from under which rock an idea may crawl.

Diverse thought creates innovative ideas.

Below are some ideas, strategies and guidelines to develop creative and innovative ideas to bridge gaps between what is desired and what is actually happening.

Brainstorming is a decision making technique in which group members present spontaneous, problem-solving suggestions to promote free, flexible, and creative thinking. It encourages group members to freely suggest alternatives, whether or not they will be used. No critical comments of any kind are allowed until all suggestions have been listed.

In the sessions, members are encouraged to think aloud, and freewheeling is welcomed. The more novel and unusual the idea, the better. The object is to promote free, flexible thinking and to enable group members to build on one another's creativity. (Daft, Marcic, 196-197)

Brainstorming is recommended to go through a three stage process.

1. **Warm-up** – terms are defined for comprehension purposes.
2. **Freewheeling** – idea generation with documentation of each and every idea.
3. **Feasibility** – the whittling down of ideas that have promise.

One company in specific, IDEO, which is responsible for the development of over 3,000 product innovations or creations at the rate of 90 per year posts these rules for brainstorming in their workplace.

1. Defer judgment
2. Build on the ideas of others
3. One conversation at a time
4. Stay focused on the topic and
5. Encourage wild ideas

Another effective and fun approach to idea generation is to choose one person to point out flaws in ideas, or in decisions. This person is the **Devil's Advocate**. The Devil's Advocate is a role set up to challenge the assumptions and assertions made by the group. The Devil's Advocate forces the group to rethink its approach to the problem and avoid reaching premature consensus or making unreasonable assumptions before proceeding with problem solutions.

Margaret Heffernan is an international business woman and author. She believes that disagreement is essential to breaking down barriers, and getting to the best solution. We must encourage disagreement? Margaret Heffernan believes we should.

Margaret Heffernan – *"Dare to Disagree"*
http://www.ted.com/talks/margaret_heffernan_dare_to_disagree.html

"When we dare to break silence or when we dare to see, when we create conflict we enable ourselves and those around us to do our very best thinking. Open information is fantastic, open networks are essential, but the truth won't set us free until we develop the skills, and the habits and the moral courage to use it. Openness isn't the end, it's the beginning." (Margaret Heffernan)

The Devil's Advocate is a delicate position to be in because it is asking another person to rethink a position or opinion that most likely they have given much thought to. The benefit is that loopholes and pitfalls are easily exposed when a Devil's Advocate is placed in the mix. This person doesn't even have to be an expert in the subject area. Sometimes, it is even better if your Devil's Advocate is looking through innocent eyes. The obvious issues that no one can see because of familiarity can come to blinding light.

Research Linking Innovation and Leadership

Innovation and leadership are like Siamese twins, they go everywhere together.

This excerpt is from a section on innovation from Kouzes and Posner's book, *The Leadership Challenge* and it explains the similarities and woven tapestry that is necessary for Leadership and Innovation to flourish. In fact, it appears that leadership is difficult without innovation and innovation is difficult without leadership.

"In Mary Beth Kanter's research, a Harvard Business professor, she investigated the human resources practices and organization designs of innovation-producing organizations. She wanted to know what fostered and what hindered innovation in the US Corporation. Our study and Kanter's were done quite independently of each other, at different periods of time, and with different purposes. We were studying leadership; Kanter was studying innovation. Yet when we

compared Kanter's cases with ours, we were struck by their similarity.
In some instances, Kanter's innovators and our leaders talked
about nearly identical projects, yet they were in completely separate
organizations in vastly different regions of the country. We and Kanter
arrived at a similar conclusion in analyzing our respective cases:
leadership is inextricably connected with the process
of innovation, of bringing new ideas, methods, or
solutions into use. *To Kanter, innovation means change,*
and "change requires leadership...a prime mover' to
push for implementation of strategic decisions."

A "Prime Mover," as Kanter described - is you. It is your role as a leader to first understand that there is a gap or potential gap and then develop a plan to close it.

> *Think of leadership without innovation and innovation*
> *without leadership as trying to start a fire without fuel,*
> *or oxygen. They are each necessary for the spark.*

An innovative, empowered environment doesn't have to look different from any other environment; it is the results that are different. The processes are often very similar, it is the way the employees feel about the process – do they own it, believe it, and want it to succeed?

> *"What made you successful in the past, won't in the future."*
> (Lew Platt, Founder of Hewlett Packard)

> *"In today's fast changing world, decisions often must be*
> *made quickly, and an organization's ability to stimulate the*
> *creativity and innovation skills of its employees is becoming*
> *increasingly important. An environment in which bosses make*
> *all the decisions and hand them down to frontline workers*
> *is becoming not only inappropriate, but inefficient."*
> (Daft, Marcic, 196)

Advantages of Participative Decision Making for Change

As we've discussed in prior chapters, participation and empowerment can change the face of an organization, department or unit. To allow as many people into the fold as possible, to share knowledge, to share ideas, and gain support all while creating an atmosphere of collaboration and teamwork is powerful.

Below are some advantages to fostering an innovative and creative workforce through participation and collaboration.

1. **Create a broader perspective** for defining the problem and diagnosing underlying causes and effects.
2. **More knowledge and facts** with which to identify potential solutions and produce more decision alternatives.
3. **More satisfaction with the decision** from the people who participate in the decision making process. They are more likely to support it.
4. **Increased support while facilitating implementation** will occur when participation is present.
5. **Reduces uncertainty for decision makers** who may be unwilling to undertake a big risk by themselves.
6. **Enhances member satisfaction** and produces support for a possibly risky situation. (Daft, Marcic, 195)

While there is power and commitment that comes from participative decision making, there are also some obstacles to consider and overcome. **Groupthink** is a phenomenon in which people are so committed to a cohesive in-group that their reluctance to express contrary opinions overrides their motivation to realistically consider alternatives. (Daft, Marcic, 196) If a group is like minded, discussion strengthens its prevailing opinions. For example, talking about racial issues increased prejudice in a high-prejudice group of high school students and decreased it in a low-prejudice group. (Myers, 565) Groupthink can occur from a lack of diversity, overconfidence from the leader, or unusually strong pressure to assimilate into a group.

Group think can be prevented by a leader who welcomes:

1. Various Opinions
2. Invite's Experts' Critique While Developing Plans
3. Assigns People to Identify Possible Problems (Myers, 566.)

"As the suppression of dissent bends a group toward bad decisions, so open debate often shapes good decisions." (David Myers)

I'll assume no further explanation is necessary to illustrate the damage Groupthink can cause.

Leading Change

Once a problem has been identified, and a solution has been foreseen, it is time to lead the change process. The change process can be looked at in two very different ways, proactive and reactive change. **Proactive change** is identifying a change initiative before it becomes a problem and creates a performance, need or process gap. Proactive change requires leaders to keep their fingers on the pulse of their area of responsibility. It lends itself to taking the time needed to ensure change can be nurtured and take root. It will also allow you to take the time to identify and remove barriers, or remove the weeds that will try to interfere with the health of your change.

Reactive change is the enemy and is a response to an event that has already occurred. The change has already taken place and reactive change is in response to a currently existing problem. Responses to reactive change can be "knee-jerk," and are often thrown at a problem to "stop the bleeding." We want our efforts in change to be proactive, not reactive.

We want our changes to address the root of the problem. This means finding the cause of the problem not symptoms of a greater problem. So often in business we become aware of a problem, the symptoms of which are obvious but it takes time to understand the root problem. So instead, we pull the weed but leave the root. Understanding comes through asking questions, taking our time, and then with understanding of the problem, taking action.

Unfortunately, as an example, we often come upon a problem, like a motorcycle accident, get out of our car and rush to the scene. We crouch down next to the cyclist. The cyclist has road rash all over. We attend to the road rash and take great care of it, when really the problem lies in the blood pulsing from the cyclist's neck. When the paramedics arrive, we say, "Look how great we took care of the road rash." The paramedics respond with, "We can see that, but he bled out from his jugular." We must identify the cause of the problem, not the symptoms. Addressing symptoms is merely identifying an effect of the problem. Our objective is to solve the problem not to hide it or ignore it.

Essential Activities Required for Leading Change

1. **Establish a sense of urgency** – identify potential crisis and opportunities.
2. **Create a guiding coalition** – a group with enough power to lead the change. Change will not take hold, if a strong enough coalition is not in place.
3. **Develop a vision and strategy** – to direct the change strategy.
4. **Communicate the change vision** - use every possible channel and opportunity to talk up and reinforce the vision and required behaviors.

5. **Empowering broad-based action** – get rid of obstacles to success, including systems and structures that constrain rather than facilitate. Encourage risk taking and experimentation.

6. **Generate short-term wins** – don't wait for the ultimate grand realization of the vision. As small victories accumulate, you make the transition from isolated initiative to an integral part of the business.

7. **Consolidate gains and produce more change** – with the well-earned credibility of previous successes, keep changing things in ways that support the vision.

8. **Anchor new approaches in the culture** – highlight positive results, communicate the connections between the new behaviors and the improved results and keep developing new change agents and leaders. (Bateman, Snell, 587)

In Summary

The ultimate goal is to establish a work environment where every person works toward something greater than themselves; something they can be proud of. It is about closing the gap between what someone needs and what someone is getting. The gap wasn't closed for the motorcyclist literally and figuratively. Change is a good thing if we look at it through the right lens. It makes our work life easier, with more control, input and decision making capacity.

Innovation is scary because it's the unknown. We've certainly all been given the chance to offer an idea and, "whammo", it goes viral. Everyone loves it. That environment could be a reality if we tap into the unfulfilled desires of employees and help them to excel like they all want to. Or we can crush ideas before they leave the tips of tongues and squelch the entire creative, spontaneous and innovative spark the group desperately needed.

To look out for each other's safety and well-being and to encourage the success of our co-workers is powerful medicine when teamwork and morale are ill. What better remedy could come than that from a workmate? Absenteeism, turnover, staffing, worker's comp and unemployment ratings would all move in the right direction on the weekly spreadsheet that monitors you, and life would be good…(I know, click your heels, Dorothy)

….but, we've had these experiences before in our lives, so we know they are possible, why not try to make it happen, again. Think about how alive you felt, looking down from the clouds, wishing you could work more…..wait, no, no, no, no…it's about working smarter, doing it with a better attitude, and doing it for the right reasons. It's about involvement. Allowing people to actively participate in their work-life and feel good about it is the goal.

Maybe it was the feeling you got talking to a parent, best friend, coach or teacher. We all want to feel better about ourselves; we all need validation for our hard work and we all need to believe in someone else. Then, it bleeds into our families and our clients, and a cultural change has taken root.

With each change, an opportunity for participation presents itself. Your job as the leader is to take that opportunity and give the team power. Ask their opinion and wade through the problems together so you all can be proud at the back-end when you solved the root problem.

CHAPTER 6

ETHICS AND RECOGNITION

A Brief History

"The time is always right to do what is right." (Martin Luther King Jr.)

Ethical decisions breed ethical decisions, and
of course, the converse is true,
unethical decisions spawn unethical decisions and cultures. It is
what we value and recognize as leaders that is perpetuated.

ETHICAL DECISION MAKING HAS BEEN mauled, squished, crushed, and put back together for millennia. Since the days of Plato who was a disciple of Socrates, and Aristotle who was a student of Plato in and around the 3rd century B.C, the question of what is right, what is wrong and what is acceptable to a given culture with given norms has been at the forefront of the debate for thousands of years. Generally, "what ought I do?" is the question that is attempted to be answered. The issue is that people see the world differently and because of this, various approaches to ethics have been developed and accepted based on a group's environment, culture, socialization and religious backgrounds. Ethics are grey, but for any given environment they should be agreed upon, communicated, practiced, enforced and recognized.

As time has unfolded and great thinkers have come and gone, a set of theories have fallen into place regarding the motivation and beliefs that allow a person to either make an ethical or unethical decision. Remember, **motivation** is an inner drive that directs a person's behavior toward goals. So then the question becomes what are the goals that motivate a person. In a workforce setting these goals can drive ethical decision making, or encourage unethical decision making. It is what the business culture values that influences the employee's decision. It is *The Infinite Space between Management and Skill Set* that a problem surfaces. The resolutions that a leader concludes, explains and solidifies create an ethical culture.

This is the link between ethics to recognition. If we recognize employees for work and decisions that are of an ethical nature, we will encourage an ethical culture to develop. If we emphasize and recognize profit over principle, we will foster an unethical environment where short cuts are made for short term gain over long term stability and reputation. How we fill the *Infinite Space between Management and Skill Set* will determine if we create an ethical or unethical culture.

But first, what are ethics? **Ethics** are the code of moral principles and values that govern the behaviors of a person or group with respect to what is right or wrong. Ethics sets standards as to what is good or bad in conduct and decision making. (Robbins, 109)

The entire point of understanding what ethics are is to understand what causes unethical behavior and what to do when one encounters an ethical dilemma. "What ought I do?" is the crux of ethics. An **ethical dilemma** arises in a situation when each alternative choice or behavior is undesirable because of potentially harmful ethical consequences. Right or wrong is not clearly defined. (Daft, Marcic, 109) Remember, ethical decision making often falls into the grey space between black and white, and right and wrong.

If you sense an ethical inconsistency, trust your gut and seek guidance.

A major consideration in making ethical decisions is whether or not our motivation is from a place of **intrinsic motivation** which calls people to action from an internal need to fulfill some outcome for personal satisfaction such as being all they can be, or helping another person for the sake of the deed. This would lend itself to an environment of ethical behavior. **Extrinsic motivation,** on the other hand, calls people to action from an external need to fulfill some outcome, such as money, power, prestige or notoriety and this can cause an unethical culture due to people acting from a suboptimum place in order to gain recognition or extrinsic rewards and often at the expense of another person, process or procedure, and for personal gain at the expense of others.

The link between ethical and unethical behavior is influenced by the culture an organization creates and what is valued and recognized by organizational leadership. We will look later at what encourages an unethical culture and what encourages an ethical culture.

Some of the ethical issues that have become prevalent in modern medicine are outlined below as well as the responsibility businesses have to maintain an ethical culture. Ethics permeate all work environments, but to examine two environments a little more closely, we will look at medical ethics and general business ethics.

"During the past three or four decades, the concerns of medical ethics expanded dramatically. This has been due both to advances in medical technology and to the desire of a better informed public to participate in medical decision making. Technological advances have driven concern beyond the physician's dilemma of being both an indispensable healer-comforter, and thereby also a favored moneymaker, to the profound dilemmas associated with womb rentals, artificial insemination, genetic engineering, behavior control, organ transplantation, human experimentation, withholding or withdrawing treatment, neonatal euthanasia, and so forth. The list goes on and on. In addition, the public - better informed, more alert to patient rights, and willing to pursue malpractice litigation – has fractured the mystique of the physician as the all-wise, not to be questioned, trusted custodian of life and death. Accordingly, moral problems associated with the doctor/ patient relationship have risen. These moral problems include informed consent, confidentiality, paternalism, truth-telling, and so forth. Increasingly, colleges of medicine have responded to this expanding

domain of medical ethics by infusing the traditional medical curriculum with courses in medical humanities." (Borchert, Stewart, 243.)

This phenomenon in medicine, as it is in business, is partly caused by the same forces that have caused the Changing Management Paradigm as we discussed in Chapter 2. With increased knowledge and education, and people desiring different things from life and work, the idea that we are equal can't help but flow into the arena of medicine and, for that matter, every other aspect of business.

> *"Governmental legislation, as well as public opinion, now requires companies to be good citizens and to be concerned for the general welfare of the community as a whole. The range of moral issues that affect a corporation's activities is vast, and is growing yearly in the public's view. These issues include the treatment of its employees, the company's role in assuring the safety and dependability of its products, its attitude toward the environment and restrictions placed upon it to prevent pollution of the air and waterways, truth in advertising, personnel policies (including affirmative action and nondiscrimination in hiring and firing decisions), plant relocation and its effect on jobs, to mention the most prevalent topics."* (Borchert, Stewart, 275, 276.)

The growing concern from society for the environment and the well-being of its customers is an on-going concern for modern business. This is referred to as **social responsibility** which, like ethics, is easy to understand: It is distinguishing right from wrong, and doing right. It means being a good corporate citizen. The formal definition is management's obligation to make choices and take actions that will contribute to the welfare and interests of society as well as the organization. (Robbins, 117)

Culture is the creator of ethical behavior.

Social responsibility has a four tiered system of operation. The first and most important tier is economic responsibility and, as you'll notice; ethical responsibility comes in third, right above the voluntary, discretionary responsibilities. Of course, ethics are irrelevant without profit and the ability to keep the doors open, but would an ethical culture create a more profitable organization? Would allowing people to be ethical and encouraging it, make them feel that they are participating in more worthwhile work? Barry Schwartz, the Dorwin Cartwright Professor of Social Theory and Social Action at Swarthmore College who frequently publishes editorials in the *New York Times* and applies his research in psychology to current events, argues, "Yes," in his lecture called, "Our Loss of Wisdom."

Barry Schwartz, "*Our Loss of Wisdom*"
http://www.ted.com/talks/lang/en/barry_schwartz_on_our_loss_of_wisdom.html

Below are the generally agreed upon levels of Social Responsibility. The question is how we collectively agree with Wall Street leering over our shoulders that the Social Responsibility Levels may need adjusted.

"We must ask, not just is it profitable, but is it right?"
(Barack Obama)

"The virtue we need above all others is practical wisdom, because it is what allows other virtues; honesty, kindness, courage and so on to be displayed at the right time and in the right way. I think people want to be allowed to be virtuous." (Barry Schwartz)

Four Tiers of Social Responsibility

1. **Economic Responsibility** – which, simply stated is, to be profitable. Nothing else matters if the business isn't profitable. This seems to inherently dictate how decisions are made in that profit is the main concern. The problem is when profit is not adequately reinvested into the organization and its employees. This causes added strain on employees and customers at the profit of investors. So many economic goals are short-term

which leads to a slow, not so gentle demise of the organization, in some cases.

2. **Legal Responsibility** – obey the law. If you obey the law because you want to and think it is right, and not because you have to, the chances of an ethical decision are greater.

3. **Ethical Responsibility** – be ethical, do what is right. Avoid harm. When profits, prestige, and power are encouraged over ethical behavior, which means people are tempted to side step ethics to gain power or position, the will of the organization, simply put, is to be profitable at any cost. This creates an untrusting, backstabbing environment where people often undermine their co-workers for their own benefit. This is a slippery slope and may work well for a few, but not the greater good.

4. **Discretionary Responsibility** – is voluntary and guided by a company's desire to make social contributions not mandated by economics, laws, or ethics. i.e. – charitable events.

As you can see ethics fall down the totem of importance. It is often difficult to maintain an ethical culture when the first question asked is, "Is this profitable?" and the second question asked is, "Is this legal?" Ethics often become an afterthought in the decision making process. The difference between legal and ethical is sometimes a fine line, but,

Not always what is legal is ethical and vice versa.

Ethics and Legality

An act can be unethical but legal or an act can be illegal but ethical. It just depends on the situation and the ethical backbone of the person viewing the situation, not to mention the organization's position on ethics. Religious or non-religious views often determine whether a person views an act as ethical or not, even if the government says the activity is legal. For example, birth control, abortion and same sex marriage, but let's look at something a little less polarizing.

Ethics and Legality

We all speed, right? We all know that it is illegal to speed, and we all know that within 7-9 miles per hour over the speed limit we are probably safe. Safe? Safe from what? Getting a ticket, or injuring another person? Generally both, so ethically we tend to agree that it is o.k. to speed within these (expanded) limits. The probability of harm at that level of law breaking is ethically worth the risk. However ethical it is, it is still illegal. Based on my commute to work – it appears that a significant majority feel that speeding a little is ethical and are willing to risk breaking the law because we've rationalized the fact that it is unlikely that significant damage would be caused to us or others.

There are many viewpoints and paradigms' surrounding the idea of ethics and what makes one person ethical and another not. Below we will look at a few of these perspectives.

Various Ethical Perspectives

"We are all changing, actualizing potentialities. Over some of these changes we have virtually no control, such as the sudden pain from a bee sting or the excretion of certain glands. Over other changes we exercise control, and we call these changes or motions voluntary. The task of ethics is to analyze and assess the nature of and conditions associated with these voluntary motions. In other words, ethics analyzes and assesses the potentialities that are open to human beings, and seeks to provide guidance for humans when they are confronted by competing, alternative potentialities." (Borchert, Stewart, 133)

With each of these various perspectives, a different approach is argued to explain the reasons people make decisions of an ethical or unethical nature, but of course that is still relative. Like leadership, motivation, communication and the various generations, everyone has different ideas, experiences, and reasons for their behavior. Ethics is no different. People see the world differently and the best and most productive way to understand why people do what they do is to learn the various reasons and thought processes behind the behavior.

Egoism is an ethical system that defines acceptable behavior as that which maximizes consequences for the individual. "Doing the right thing," the focus of moral philosophy, is defined by egoism as, "do the act that promotes the greatest good for oneself." If everyone follows this system, the well-being of society as a whole should increase. (Bateman, Snell, 143)

The issue with this perspective is that if everyone looks out for their own self-interest, there is no group or team, just individuals. This philosophy develops more readily in a capitalistic society but is unsustainable for the overall well-being of the whole. If it were practical then humans would never have joined in small bands of people and the exchange of ideas that sparked innovation and rapid technology advancement, would not have occurred. This philosophy seems counter intuitive to what we know about human behavior and development.

Egoism and the Invading Army

Imagine an egoist is propositioned with this ethical dilemma – a foreign army has landed on American soil and is coming through town. The army's leader captures you. They explain that they are going to wipe out everyone in its path, except you. Or, they give you're the option to sacrifice yourself and save thousands of people from perishing.

An egoist would say that they will let everyone else die, because their life is as important as or more important than everyone else's. The action works for them, regardless as to what happens to everyone else.

I'll do what's right, right for me.

Utilitarianism is an ethical system that believes that decisions should be made with the greatest good in mind. It is nearly opposite of Egoism. This means that for a decision to be ethically sound, the greatest number of people would benefit from the decision even if a few had to suffer.

Utilitarianism and the Invading Army

Given the example of the army invading from above, a Utilitarian would sacrifice themselves for the greater good of the community with the idea that at least one person who was spared would have a greater impact on the well-being of the group and for certain all the people kept alive would have a greater positive effect than just one person left in place of the whole.

The utilitarianism philosophy encourages groups to look out for one another and the greater good. This system requires courage.

Courage isn't being fearless, it is overcoming fear in the face of danger.

Relativism is based on the opinions and behaviors of other people within the person's sphere of influence. The relativist holds that there are only the norms that a particular society sets up, and these norms vary greatly from one society to another. (Borchert, Stewart, 68) A **norm** is a shared belief about how people should think and behave. (Bateman, Snell, 450.)

Relativism and the Invading Army

To a relativist in the invading army the scenario we mentioned above may play out like this: The person in the ethical dilemma would consult other people or experts, regarding norms and expectations of the cultural group and make a decision based on input from others as to which course of action most aligns with the norms of the group. They may conclude that all life is precious and to collectively fight, or they may decide to just surrender and see.

The best evidence to support this perspective is that different cultures around the world have very different ideas as to what is right and wrong. It is the environment, the people, the norms and expectations of a culture that dictate ethical lines of behavior. Some cultures are still cannibals, others don't eat beef, while some won't touch swine.

If the group thinks it is best and it is in-line with
our norms, we'll take that action.

Determinism states that humans do not have free choice, that every event is precipitated by an event which makes a person act. There are no other possible alternatives to the decision making process. It has already been decided based on the cause driving one to act.

Determinism and the Invading Army

A determinist would possibly say, "What's meant to be will be. If I'm the one the army chooses to spare, then it wasn't my time to go. There's a plan for everyone. I'll just sit back and wait to see." This unfortunately is a very passive and defeatist approach to decision making and life in general.

If we have no control and everything is going to happen the way it is going to happen, then why care about it or anything else? If something good was to happen to us, we would not be able to feel any sense of ownership to the event or pride in accomplishing something good. Likewise, on the contrary, if something bad happens, or you do something bad, it wasn't your fault, it was already determined to be.

It doesn't matter. It's out of my control.

Moral Rights perspective believes that human beings should not have fundamental rights infringed upon or taken away due to an ethical decision. If those rights are abridged the moral rights advocate believes the decision is unethical. Thus, an ethically correct decision is one that best maintains the rights of those people affected by it. (Daft, Marcic, 112)

Some of the moral rights that are considered during the decision making process are;

1. **The right of free consent** – Individuals are to be treated only as they knowingly and freely consent to be treated.
2. **The right to privacy** – individuals can choose to do as they please away from work and have control of information about their private lives.

3. **The right to freedom of conscience** – individuals may refrain from carrying out any order that violates their moral or religious norms.

4. **The right to free speech** – individuals may criticize truthfully the ethics or legality of actions of others.

5. **The right to due process** – individuals have a right to an impartial hearing and fair treatment.

6. **The right to life and safety** – individuals have a right to live without endangerment or violation of their health and safety.

This is the most applicable approach to developing an ethical culture within a work group or organization. It provides guideposts for decision making and takes into account the very nature of ethical decision making. It provides rights to those who are affected by the decisions and gives the decision maker's checkpoints to ensure a violation in ethics does not occur. In the invading army scenario, we would analyze the intent of the invading army and if no one's rights were being violated, we'd consider it ok, but if they were infringed, we'd have to take action. Generally, an invading army would violate our rights and we would have to act.

It is every human being's right to be treated ethically.

Justice approach states that moral decisions must be based on standards of equity, fairness, and impartiality. (Daft, Marcic, 112) This approach coupled with the moral rights approach is a strong ally in the development of an ethically sound workforce. It is also the most closely aligned with that of a learning organization and the principles and fundamentals we have discussed thus far. To look deeper into the justice approach, there are three types of justice, leaders should be concerned with:

1. **Distributive justice** – requires that different treatment of people must not be based on arbitrary reasons. Individuals who are similar in respects relevant to a decision should be treated similarly.

2. **Procedural Justice** – means that rules must be administered fairly. They should be stated concisely and clearly and should be impartially enforced.

3. **Compensatory Justice** – argues that individuals should be compensated for the cost of their injuries by the party responsible. (Daft, Marcic, 113)

It is the leader's role to determine the ethical guideposts of their area of responsibility, above and beyond the organization's standards.

"Managers bring specific personality and behavioral traits to the job. Personal needs, family influence, and religious background all shape a manager's value system." (Daft, Marcic, 114)

Ethics

I was the Head of HR for many years in hospital systems and physician groups. Eventually, because of the unethical decisions I encountered and often had to combat at my own peril, left healthcare. Patients were discharged before they were ready because the hospital wasn't paid past a certain Medicare/Medicaid established timeline based on the patient's condition. Procedures in the Cath lab were done when they were not necessary. Doctors were recruited and paid beyond the fair market value to run out other groups. Nothing was about the patient. The executive teams I was part of climbed over one another to make a name for themselves at the expense of anyone who got in their way. I felt like I was going to have a heart attack.

My head pounded like all the blood in my body tried to cram into my skull. I went to a cardiologist to have a stress test. The doctor said, "You're going to die someday, but it won't be because of your heart." I explained the environment I worked in. He concluded the stress and my blood pressure were caused from work. He prescribed what he called, "a chill pill." It was a non-addictive, non-controlled substance called Buspirone. It was for anxiety!

I hated that I had to take that pill. I was always cool under pressure – had been my whole life. I did yoga and meditated, but it only swatted away the flies of stress and anxiety from the trash heap I walked into at the physician group in Florida. The pill was a Band-Aid to stop the black little pebble in my chest cavity from shriveling up and dying. It was to slow the vacuum in my mind from exhausting my soul. I needed out.

We moved from Florida, back to my home city of Cincinnati. I took the severance for three months from a Goldman Sachs portfolio company who recruited me to "take over the anesthesia world," only to find out that after three months, Goldman was going to sell the company.

I sat in a garage outside of Cincinnati for 6 months and took hammer to chisel, blow torch to metal and created sculptures. I stopped taking my chill pills, continued with yoga and meditation and contemplated my future. I had about 30 pieces picked up by two galleries. Eventually, I decided that I missed working with people, missed or more accurately, desperately needed the income and started my job search. I wasn't looking for a publicly traded company. I had done that. I wasn't looking at healthcare. I landed at a Group of Companies – all three were in the construction industry.

*Shortly after I started, I was in one of the partner's offices with a project superintendent. They discussed a concrete pour that needed to be redone. It was going to cost the company $100,000 dollars. The conversation was amazing – there was no blame tossed around. The Partner didn't try to pin it on the subcontractor, superintendent, or anyone else. It was a pleasant, problem solving conversation. Then, in one sentence, I heard more f-bombs than I heard in a public venue in healthcare, ever. The partner and owner, a former superintendent, said, "I don't give a f*ck. We're going to tear that m*ther f*cker out and do the f*cking thing right! That's all I want to f*cking hear about that!" I knew immediately that I could work for this guy and this company. I knew I had found my home.*

Ethics takes many forms. In healthcare we had codes of conduct that forbade that language, but we created a culture that encouraged short cuts and took advantage of patients. It's interesting how the for profit - corporate world elevates themselves and hides behind petty corporate codes of morality, and then without batting an eye, has no problem taking advantage of someone in need for a profit. The culture that the partner of a $200,000,000 million dollar construction company created and then *demonstrated with incredible clarity was why clients came back, year after year, and company growth stayed steady, even during the mid-2000's recession. Regardless of the language, his attitude and ethical compass was dead set on morality.*

Not only are the Moral Rights and Justice Approaches consistent with business norms, they are consistent with business law and our world of work. They both squarely give the leader and the people involved a basis for developing, controlling and changing the ethical cultures within their organization. For a leader to influence the ethical underpinnings of an organization, it is important to understand the ethical development people progress through. This way you will be able to determine which level of ethical development you will be dealing with, given a certain individual or group, and even assess where you are as a leader.

Personal Moral Development

The diagram and passage is based on Lawrence Kohlberg's work and it has been taken from the Third Edition of *Understanding Management* by Richard Daft, and Dorothy Marcic. Kohlberg divided the Personal Moral Development of human beings into three distinct levels.

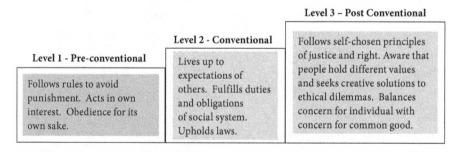

Level 3 – Post Conventional

Follows self-chosen principles of justice and right. Aware that people hold different values and seeks creative solutions to ethical dilemmas. Balances concern for individual with concern for common good.

Level 2 - Conventional

Lives up to expectations of others. Fulfills duties and obligations of social system. Upholds laws.

Level 1 - Pre-conventional

Follows rules to avoid punishment. Acts in own interest. Obedience for its own sake.

Level 1 or Pre-Conventional Stage - (Extrinsically Motivated) of moral development finds people concerned with external rewards and punishments, and they obey authority to avoid detrimental personal consequences. In an organizational context, this level may be associated with managers who use an autocratic or coercive leadership style, with employees oriented toward dependable accomplishment of specific tasks. This is the behavior of a child, "Will I get in trouble or not?" It isn't about right or wrong, it's about consequences.

Level 2 or Conventional Stage – (Extrinsically Motivated) people learn to conform to the expectations of good behavior as defined by colleagues, family, friends, and society. Meeting social and interpersonal obligations is important. Work group collaboration is the preferred manner for accomplishment of organizational goals, and managers use a leadership style that encourages interpersonal relationships and cooperation. Most people are at this level of ethics.

Level 3 or Post-Conventional Stage – (Intrinsically Motivated) of moral development finds that individuals are guided by an internal set of values and standards and will even disobey rules or laws that violate these principles. Internal values become more important than the expectations of significant others. 20% of people operate at this level of ethics.

Post Conventional Ethics

When the USS Indianapolis sank after being torpedoed during WWII, one Navy pilot disobeyed orders and risked his life to save men who were being picked off by sharks. The pilot operated from the highest level of moral development when he attempted the rescue despite a direct order from his superiors. He would have rather risked his own life, than stand idle and watch his friends die.

Life, experience, religion and philosophy dictated how he reacted to that ethical situation. His decision would have been well thought out and he likely would have felt that any other course of action would be unethical. His own personal ethics superseded that of the commanding officers and he went above and beyond what the organization's ethical guideposts were or the commanding officer's.

He was ready to accept the consequences for his actions even at his own peril. He likely had a utilitarian approach to ethics. People in the pre and conventional stages of ethics, would likely not have even identified the situation as an ethical dilemma.

When leaders operate from the highest level of development, they use transformative or servant leadership (as discussed in Chapter 1, The Differences Between Leadership and Management) focusing on the needs of followers and encouraging others to think for themselves and to engage in higher levels of moral reasoning. Employees are empowered and given opportunities for constructive participation in governance of the organization. The great majority of managers operate at level two. A few have not advanced beyond level one. Only about 20% of American adults reach the level three stage of moral development. People at level three are able to act in an independent, ethical manner regardless of expectations from others inside or outside the organization. Managers at level three of moral development will make ethical decisions no matter what the organizational consequences are for them. (Daft, Marcic, 114-115)

Guidelines for Ethical Decision Making

When we are deliberating about whether or not to make a decision because of moral or ethical issues, we often ask ourselves how a significant person in our life may respond to the decision, or we may even ask ourselves if we will be able to sleep at night. These are our own internal guideposts for decision making. I'm sure many of us have said to ourselves,

I'm the one who has to live with myself.

Of course this means you want the decision to be a good one; one you can be proud of and feel good talking to others about. In addition to the personal beacons we all have, the guidelines below for ethical decision making will whittle down the concerns one may have before they get to the other side of a tough ethical decision. These will not tell us exactly what to do or how to do it, but they will help bring to light some tough considerations during the process of making an ethical decision.

1. **Don't make assumptions** - Is the problem/dilemma really what it appears to be? If you are not sure, find out.

2. **Is it legal/ethical** - if you are not sure the action you are taking is legal and/or ethical, ask someone.

3. **How will you feel** – if you take an action? If guilt, doubt, remorse, worry or trepidation are involved, it's likely a good indication that your gut is telling you it is not wise.

4. **Is it reasonable** – do you understand the position of those who oppose the action you are considering?

Remember, you can't counter or respond to a person's
point until you know their point of view.

5. **What are the effects** – who does the action benefit, harm, and for how long and how much.

6. **Transferability** – Would you be willing to allow everyone to do what you are considering doing?

7. **Consult experts** – Have you sought the opinion of others who are knowledgeable on the subject and who would be objective?

8. **Are you proud of the decision** – would your action be embarrassing to you if it were made known to your family, friends, co-workers or superiors? If you wouldn't tell your mother, it's probably not a good idea.

Warning Signs of an Unethical Culture

People often give in to what they perceive to be pressures or preferences of powerful others. Professor, Arthur Brief of Tulane University states, "If the boss says, 'Achieve a specific sales or profit target, period.' I think, people will do their very best to achieve those directions even if it means sacrificing their own values. They may not like it, but they define it as part of the job." (Bateman, Snell, 148)

With this, it is very clear that ethical behavior starts at the top and is pushed down. The key is that everyone in the organization, especially the executive leaders, are pushing a culture down that is ethical, socially responsible and in-line with the expectations of the environment.

In organizations, it is an on-going challenge to maintain consistent ethical behavior by all employees. What are some danger signs that an organization may be allowing or even encouraging unethical behavior among its people?

Unethical Cultural Warning Signs

1. Excessive emphasis on short term revenues over longer-term considerations.
2. Failure to establish a written code of ethics.
3. A desire for simple, "quick fix" solutions to ethical problems.
4. An unwillingness to take an ethical stand that may impose financial costs.
5. Consideration of ethics solely as a legal issue or a public relations tool.
6. Lack of clear procedures for handling ethical problems.
7. Response to the demands of shareholders at the expense of other considerations. (Bateman, Snell, 148)

Using Recognition and Positive Reinforcement to Develop an Ethical Culture

After digging into the nature of ethical decision making, the fundamentals of how people make ethical decisions and how human moral development occurs, it is apparent that we as leaders have a considerable amount of control regarding the environment we create in our worlds of work. Again, *the Infinite Space between* ethical issue identification, and ethical decision making is where the culture is created. How leaders act, respond, and speak is critical. All eyes are on you, all the time.

We discussed reinforcement in the section on Motivation. There were four types of reinforcement used to change a person's behavior; punishment, extinction, avoidance learning and positive reinforcement. The first three are more or less negative approaches to changing a person's behavior. What we are going to focus on is the positive reinforcement or recognition for desired behavior. **Positive Reinforcement** is to actively give pleasant and positive feedback for a desired behavior whether verbal, or another form.

If for example, an organization recognizes or rewards employees for getting the job done below budget, the likelihood of employees working to keep the project under budget will become paramount because that is what the emphasis is on. With a focus like this, employees may be more inclined to cut corners, use suboptimum supplies, and inevitably, quality will suffer.

What you focus on as a leader is what your followers will also focus on.

On the other hand, if an organization such as a hospital rewards or recognizes employees for compliments, positive patient comments, teamwork, collaboration, improved patient satisfaction scores or quality outcomes, the likelihood of employees focusing their attention on these items is greater which in turn, should positively affect the bottom line. We often take an upside down approach which is to say we focus on making money at any cost and then focus on doing it right. This approach creates a lot of work at the back-end, once the culture has been created, to regain the confidence of employees and customers.

As the leader, be the culture you want to create –
live it, practice it and tell people about it. Fill the Infinite
Space between Management and Skill Set with what
you want ethically, and the organization needs.

Recognition for a job well done is not only a great motivator to continue to perform at high levels, but it is a terrific source of self-esteem. Remember, for an employee to reach self-actualization, they need to have high self-esteem according to Maslow. Often leaders feel like their employees are "just doing what they are paid to do." That is the truth but, as a leader, if you want to encourage continued affirmative behavior, recognition will provide the vehicle for higher satisfaction, and improved performance. In one study done by Dr. Bob Nelson, President of Nelson Motivation Inc., "Workers were asked to rank a list of motivators from 1-10 in order of importance."

- Workers rated 'appreciation for a job well done,' as the #1 motivator; supervisors ranked it #8.
- Employees ranked 'feeling in on things,' as the #2 in importance; Their managers ranked it #10." (Nelson)

Again, this is a very good illustration of the gaps that sometimes exist between leaders and employees. One of our jobs as leaders is to close gaps. How we fill these gaps is the critical aspect to leadership. If employees want recognition for a job well done and want to feel, "in on things," which means communication and empowerment, then we as leaders must give them what they need. While at the same time, we as leaders must create an environment conducive to teamwork, accountability, high morale and lower turnover.

Keys to Positive and Effective Recognition

It is advisable for each unit leader to develop attainable and measurable goals. These goals should reflect the larger organization's goals and the two should feed each other with energy. The guidelines below will help you ensure your efforts in recognition toward ethical behavior are not wasted.

1. **Instantaneous Recognition** – reward the behavior when it happens, timing is very important, don't delay praise. DON'T WAIT...TAKE THE TIME! Example; "I see you are in a meeting with Pat...however I wanted to let you know the way you responded to Dr. Smith today was very impressive! When you are done here can we talk in my office?"

2. **Be Sincere** – Words seem hollow if you are not sincere in why you're praising. Eye contact...body language...STOP...don't keep walking...take the time! TONE OF VOICE. So often leaders say things in passing or with their hand on the door. This sends a poor message. Ask them to come to your office or go to them specifically to tell them good job. Especially do this if the only time they usually see you is because of criticism or when a problem arises.

3. **Be Specific** – Avoid generalizations in favor of details of the achievement or action. This gives the act of praise more meaning. It gives the recognizable deed more relevance. Again be specific... "Lisa I was glad I was in the department this morning to hear how you explained Mrs. Jones' imaging procedure to her. You were able to put her at ease and obviously made her feel better about the process."

4. **Personal Praise** – When possible, convey your praise in person, face to face. Technology is a wonderful thing...however...not in this instance.

5. **Be Positive and Stay Positive** – do not undercut praise with a concluding note of criticism. Take the opportunity of the situation and make it a positive. Do not do this... "Marge you did an excellent job handling Mr. Johnson's issues. Those anti-depressants must really be working."

6. **Be Proactive** – Praise progress toward goals, otherwise you'll tend to react to the negative – typically mistakes – in your interactions with others.

No one ever gets tired of hearing thank you.

Creating Positive Feedback

When you give someone feedback, or praise, it is important that the person walks away feeling good about it. The worst case scenario is that the employee walks away feeling patronized or pacified. To ensure your attempts at recognition are valuable, following these basic guidelines as described by Dr. Bob Nelson.

1. **I saw what you did** – the employee doesn't know what you see, but if you explain to them exactly why what they did was so powerful, they will be encouraged to continue that behavior. It is an opportunity to use clear, concise language to have a very positive conversation.

*I saw you walking around the job and as you passed each person,
you stopped to see if anyone needed anything.*

2. **I appreciate what you did** – place value on the behavior or achievement. Explain how what the employee did pushed the employee closer to meeting the agreed upon goals. For example,

*I appreciate you doing that because it demonstrates teamwork,
and that you are concerned with your people.*

3. **Explain why it is important** – provide context to the situation, and illustrate how the action may have affected others on the periphery of the situation or how it was important to operations, goals, or the team. For example,

*This is important because it demonstrates to others that
we are all in this together, and it illustrates to staff that
you are truly there for them. You set a good example.*

4. **Here's how it made me feel** – give an emotional charge. Explain how what they did made you feel or how it made another person feel.

*I was proud of your work yesterday. You made me feel very
good about having you working in our company.
I know you'll keep the best interests of our clients in mind.
You're a good superintendent. These folks are
lucky to have you looking out for them.*

Ideas for Recognition and Involvement Programs

A few years back, 1,500 employees were surveyed in a variety of work settings to find out what they considered to be the most powerful workplace motivator. Their response? Recognition, recognition, recognition! (Robbins, 192)

Employee recognition programs can consist of giving approval, personal attention, expressing interest and, of course, appreciation for excellent work. At the BIC Corporation in Milford, Connecticut, which makes pens, razors and cigarette lighters, production employees meet every week to review offerings from the employee suggestion box. Whenever a group voices its support for a proposal, it is immediately passed on to the appropriate supervisor, who has 10 days to put the change in place. (Robbins, 193)

Active Leadership

Being an active, engaged leader is the most important aspect of leading the recognition initiative. You must be visible, approachable and open to suggestions with a non-biased attitude. Employees must feel as if you are their ally in process improvement, teamwork, participation and communication. The employee must feel no hesitation when they have an idea or concern to share with you.

Tips for Presenting Yourself as an Active Leader

1. **Walk around** - get to know each employee personally.
2. **Emphasize the positive** – focus your attention on what employees do well.
3. **Use negatives as an opportunity** – when something goes wrong, use it as an opportunity to teach the employee, not scold. This will make employees more open to be creative and find solutions if they know you will be a resource for them.
4. **Listen** – when an employee approaches you, listen to them fully. Do not rebut, or interrupt – let them get to their point. Refer to Chapter Two on Communication for ideas.

Suggestion Box

In no way will the following be as effective as the prior suggestion, but they are a good supplement to solid, active leadership. This gives employees a say in their work. It is recommended that even if the larger organization has a suggestion box, a department specific suggestion box still be used. It also sets the stage for people to avoid complaining unless they are willing to make a suggestion for improvement. Some ideas for implementing a unit specific suggestion box are:

1. **Discuss suggestions as a group** – let the group weigh in on the validity of the idea and let the group figure out how it will work, or won't work.
2. **Implement suggestions as a team** – once an idea has been accepted, discuss as a group who will do what and how. Let assignments be divided out by the group.
3. **Recognize the author** – when a suggestion is used, recognize the idea generator publicly.

Recognition Board

This provides a place for employees, patients, customers, and other co-workers to see how well others are doing. It may also inspire others to change their behavior so they can find themselves on the recognition board. Some companies are moving to a Intranet sites which are essentially the employees company website that only employees can access. This is a great venue to post recognition to. Again, even if the organization as a whole has a recognition board, try setting up a unit specific board. Be sure to consider these factors as you move forward.

1. **Public** – recognize employees so others can see how great they are.
2. **Different People** – ensure different people are responsible for updating the board and changing the format of the board, maybe with seasonal themes, etc. This will create a sense of community, that everyone is responsible and encourage more pride in the effort.
3. **Recognize the Small Things** – as well as the big things. Recognition for both small and large deeds encourages others to follow suit and behave in ways that are favorable to the goals

of the department which ultimately should provide satisfaction to employees because they helped develop the goals.

Tokens of Appreciation

A token of appreciation could be a thank you note. Many companies have their own Intranet sites which are great platforms for this activity. It isn't uncommon for people to hang them in their workspace to show them off. If everyone knows what they are, they gain more interest and attention. Refer to Creating Positive Feedback and Keys to Positive and Effective Recognition in this section to ensure you don't leave any opportunity unstoked. The tokens of appreciation could also be stickers, or even small monetary awards, gift certificates and the like.

The advantage to implementing these strategies is that people will begin to self-monitor themselves. They will know what is expected, what they need to do to thrive and how they need to do it. Remember, the more employees that can work independently and handle their business with critical thinking skills and make the right decision within the policy and procedural guidelines of the organization, the more time you as the leader will have to focus on bringing people up to their maximum potential and do what every leader is charged with doing – creating inspiration.

Developing an Ethical Culture through Goals and Recognition

No matter what the organizational goals are, the department goals should enhance and perpetuate the attainment of the overall organizational goals. The department goals should also be attainable and easily measured. Employees should be able to monitor the attainment of goals and have direct impact on reaching the departmental goal which will feed the organizational goals.

To ensure that these goals are agreeable to employees, attainable, specific and measurable, develop these goals as a group. This process will give the employees power to affect their own work-life. Empowerment is a critical aspect in the attainment of goals. Employees need to feel like they have control over the success or failure of goal attainment. If a leader and team develop mutually acceptable goals, the likelihood that employees will buy-in, commit and make it happen is greater. There shouldn't be too many goals at once because people get bogged down and lose focus especially if they are being pulled in different directions.

Fix one problem at a time and do it well.
Don't attempt multiple priorities at once and
expect anything but mediocre results.

Once a goal has been attained, celebrate and recognize those that contributed to the success. Each time you as the leader see an employee working toward the goal, acknowledge them and tell them, "good job." Fill *the Space between* goal development and goal attainment with positive reinforcement. This will encourage them to continue the behavior, and it helps their self-esteem. It will eliminate ambiguity and allow people to feel good about their work, knowing that what they are doing is bigger than them. It will remind them that they do have important and meaningful jobs.

Remember, the goals should be in-line ethically with the organization, your department and what you are trying to accomplish. The goals should be measurable issues that will create a culture of ethical behavior not tempt people to be unethical. Focus on small things like communicating quickly and often with clients by returning calls as soon as possible. **"Answer the Why,"** and explain to them that the quicker we respond to a call the more pleasant the client will be and the more pleasant the employee's work day will be. Remember, the investment at the front-end of an experience will make the back-end run smoother. Goals like this will encourage a culture of care, and motivation for the right reasons. They may even get to go home to their families with good attitudes which then can turn into a cycle of positivity which bleeds back into their work-life.

CHAPTER 7

TIME MANAGEMENT

"Half our life is spent trying to find something to do with the time we have rushed through life trying to save." Yale Richmond

You can make more money, but you can't make more time.

A Brief Introduction

I HAVE SEEN THE WAY people feel about certain leaders change from positive and supportive to negative and obstinate because of one issue that manifests into a bunch of little symptoms that drive people bonkers. "He never show's up on time. We'll see him 20 minutes late. He never returns emails. He can't make a decision. You can't talk to him about anything – he can't focus. He's always thinking of something else. He can't decide what he wants to do. What does he even do? He says "yes" to everything."

I'm sure we all have firsthand encounters with these people or have heard the stories about them. Generally, people are pretty accommodating, understanding and supportive, but once the relationship becomes a one way street, things change. People become aggravated and begin to take things personally. Inevitably, the principle of reciprocity begins to creep into the situation. For example, if someone doesn't show up to a meeting on-time, doesn't submit assignments on-time or disregards emails, there will be a price. The cost is loss of respect, loss of influence and a loss of cohesion in groups.

Time is something we all share, but some people do not think twice about stealing it from us if they need more even if it's due to their own mismanagement of time. Make no mistake about it, someone that is not respectful of our time, IS stealing from us.

I cannot begin to tell you how many times I've encountered a leader that can't seem to understand that their decisions regarding the way they spend their time is at the root of their own success and failure. Well, more accurately stated, people attribute their success to themselves, but rarely attribute their failures in the same way, but often attribute their failure to external forces. This is called the **Self-Serving Bias** which will be discussed further in Chapter 10. This is a symptom of poor time management. People say, "I work 50 hours a week." My first thought is, "you need to prioritize and work more efficiently." Most people respond with, "Man, you are overworked." It's not uncommon for people with poor time management skills to blame others for their short-comings. Why? They can't say no. They can't delegate. They can't make a decision. They can't focus on the main points at hand and are easily distracted by the next shiny object. They can't organize. When you ask them, "What are your goals? What are you trying to accomplish? In what order do you want these things to take place?" Their answer has not been thought out, but they've also not likely considered the correct order or what the goal is because they can't step back to prioritize and develop a plan because they are treading water in a pool, going nowhere, except slowly down. We have to eliminate the noise and clutter in our mind to see clearly.

"Silence is essential. We need silence, just as much as we need air, just as much as plants need light. If our minds are crowded with words and thoughts there is no space for us." (Thich Nhat Hanh)

Poor time management is like treading water in a dirty pond, while all along you feel and act like you are racing in a crystal clear pool in the Olympics' finals.

Improving time management starts with seeing that your own decisions are the reasons you can't seem to manage your own schedule.

"The bad news is time flies. The good news is you're the pilot." (Michael Altshuler)

Assessing Poor Time-Management Skills

Admitting you have poor time management skills is like admitting you have a drinking problem. Often there isn't a problem to the person with poor time management until they see it and acknowledge it, or it becomes such a problem to those around them, that they have to address it or risk damaging or losing relationships. It may be a problem to everyone around them, but until it becomes a problem for them, they are blind, and just like an alcoholic, will blame everyone and everything around them for their issues with Time Management. Now, Time Management isn't a disease, but the same denial occurs with both alcoholism and time management.

I'm late because I was on a call with another person. No, you're late because you either didn't plan enough time for the call or between the call and meeting, or you weren't able to tell the person on the call you had a meeting, or you just decided that the person on the call was more important than the people waiting on you. Either way, none of the issues are caused by anyone but yourself and no one thinks you are overworked. They just think you don't respect their time, or they feel like you are unorganized and scattered. Either is not good.

The 11 Symptoms of Poor Time Management https://www.coachingpositive performance.com/11-symptoms-poor-time-management/

As you read through these, put a little check next to the items that you seem to run into over the course of the week. Be honest. Acknowledgement is the first step to recovery. I know that's a little heavy, but you get the point.

1. ☐ **Poor Punctuality** – we find ourselves regularly late for appointments. Regardless if we feel our excuse is legit or not,

others around us will grow weary. Poor punctuality impacts others and, as a result, usually has a negative impact on the quality of relationships. It is better to decline a meeting rather than accept it and show up late. At least the expectations are established.

2. ☐ **Rushing** – Are we constantly rushing from one apppointment to another? The occasional rush is not a problem, but if it's a regular occurrence, more than one time per week, check the box. Constantly rushing is often a sign that we are struggling with overwhelm and overload. We need to focus on getting more work off our plate by saying 'No," delegating, automating, and outsourcing.

Delegation requires trust and confidence in the person we delegate to.
This is a compliment and show of commitment.
Delegate so others can grow.

3. ☐ **Impatience** – can be an indicator of poor time management skills. Maybe there wasn't enough time scheduled between meetings or for meetings to run over (which should be avoided.) Often people project the things they do not like about themselves on to other people. Impatience is often the first sign that we have poor time management skills. We take our failings out on others. If we are becoming more impatient, it is time to examine our workload and work practices.

4. ☐ **Poorly Defined Goals** – When we wake up in the morning to go to work, do we know what the major issues of our day will be? Do we know what the minor issues are? What major projects are we working on? When are they due? If this isn't clear to us, or those around us, refine our goals and prioritize them so our time is spent most effectively. Lists are good ways to determine tasks and their importance.

Remember from Ch. 4 Motiovation, goals must be:

A. **Must be acceptable to and agreed upon by the employee**

B. **Challenging but attainable**
C. **Specific, quantifiable, and measurable**

5. ☐ **Procrastination** – People put off the things they don't like doing. Therefore, to avoid this as a career inhibitor, do these things first, not last when we are tired and don't want to do them. Deadlines will be missed and quality will suffer otherwise. Ask ourselves...

> *What is the most important task I can complete*
> *with the time and resources available to me?*

When taking on procrastination, we must be sure that the task/project we are putting off actually needs to be done. There is no benefit to making time for tasks/projects which add no value to our work or life.

> *Often we assign importance inappropriately*
> *because we "prefer" one task over another.*

The Three Forms of Procrastination

Approximately 20 percent of people are chronic procrastinators; for them, the behavior cuts across all domains of life. But some people procrastinate in specific situations.

- **Arousal types**, or thrill-seekers, wait until the last minute in order to reap a euphoric rush.
- **Avoiders** put off tasks because of fear of failure or even fear of success; in either case, they are highly concerned with what others think of them.
- **Decisional** procrastinators struggle to make decisions; for them, not making a decision absolves them of responsibility for the outcome of events. Unfortunately this also provides no direction or leadership and often people muddle around in the grey space of uncertainty

and paralysis which simply exacerbates the already problematic situation with Time Management.

Whichever the type, there are big costs to procrastination: It is internally troubling, potentially leading to problems such as insomnia and immune system and gastrointestinal disturbances, and it erodes personal relationships and teamwork in the workplace. https://www.psychologytoday.com/us/basics/procrastination

6. ☐ **Poor Performance** – We can get away with poor Time Management for awhile, but eventually it catches up to us. We begin to miss deadlines; we are constantly late for appointments and our impact on other people becomes too much for them to cope with. Our productivity levels decline and our backlog increases. Too many people think high performance is about getting large amounts of work done, but quantity is not as important as we might think. If we are getting a lot of work done but that work is unimportant, or not reaping rewards, are we really performing to a high level? No. Hell No!

*"Most people overstimate what they can do in a month
and underestimate what they can do in an hour."*

Performance, Effort and Results

I played high school football with a guy who really wanted to be a wide-receiver. He was fast, he ran hard and he had all the drive in the world to be successful. Our coach entertained his idea of being a wide-out. He jumped in the rotation with the rest of us and ran routes, and had passes thrown to him.

This guy ran great routes, and looked good doing it. The summer before football two-a-days began, he ran at the track and his dad threw him passes. The guy was committed to being a wide receiver. He told us all about it. In fact, he talked about it all the time as if we weren't committed. We however, had one critical thing going for us, that he did not.

We ran the drills at practice. The receivers went out, caught the balls and returned them. He did the same thing, except the ball hit off his hands, bounced of his chest, hell, one hit him in the face mask. The coach finally said, "go over there with the defensive backs and work on tackling." The guy looked at our coach and said, "coach I work as hard or harder than anyone else on this field." The coach said, "effort only matters if it produces results."

It doesn't matter how fast you are, or how hard you work or how open you can get, if everything you do ends in a dropped pass. If you can't catch, you can't be a receiver. The bottom line is, quantity doesn't matter no matter how much effort is put forth if the effort and quantity of effort doesn't reap quality results. Would this player have been better off understanding his strengths and weaknesses and focusing on his strenghts to maximize his effort? Would he have used his time more wisely by prioritizing differently nd focusing on tackling rather than a skill set he simply could not develop?

> *Don't mistake effort and time spent working*
> *with quality and/or high performance.*

7. ☐ **Lack of Energy** – When we have poor time managerment skills, we are constantly chasing our tail. We fall behind on tasks and we have to work extra hard to catch up. Eventually, our energy levels begin to drop and we lose motivation. It becomes harder to catch up and so we fall further behind which drains us of even more energy.

Energy management is just as important as time management. In fact, the two go hand in hand. Organizing our time is wonderful but if we don't have the energy to do anything, time management is irrelevant. Poor time management can come about because we haven't been managing our energy levels effectively. Due to lack of energy, it takes longer to get everything done and we start to fall behind in our work which then puts us under pressure, drains us of more energy and takes up more of our time.

It can become a downward spiral if not managed. Poor energy levels could be because of lack of sleep, because we stay up late to get things done that should have been done during the work day. We stay up late and then wake up exhausted and unprepared to tackle the next day which then only exacerbates the poor performance and buries us further.

Running a marathon without sleep or with low energy levels will affect your performance, just like lack of sleep or energy will lower your productivity and ability to think and plan.

8. ☐ **Perfectionism** – We spend so much time trying to prepare and make sure that we perform the task perfectly that we either fail to start or go incredibly slow. In reality, very few tasks are ever performed perfectly, but when we are overcome by a need for perfection, it can be hard to see that.

Let Perfection Go

In the entire history of Olympic gymnastics there have only been 6 perfect 10's. The first was in 1976 and the last was in 1992. These gymnasts are the best in the world and only six times have they reached their goal of perfection.

You can still win a gold and not be perfect – let perfect go and in it's place find the sweet spot between quantity and quality so you can remain positively productive.

Even a job done to an average standard is better than a perfect job which never gets done.

Warning Signs of Perfectionism

- **You think in all-or-nothing terms.** Something is either right or wrong, good or bad, perfect or a disaster. For example, you tend to think, "She is mean," instead of, "She can sometimes be mean.
- **You can't trust others to do a task correctly**, so you rarely delegate.

144

- **You think, and then act, in extremes**. Have you ever acted on a sentiment like this, more than once? "I had one cookie and screwed up my <u>diet</u>...I might as well eat them all."
- **You have demanding standards for yourself and others**. You believe in always giving your best and you expect others to do the same. You are scared to death of looking like a failure.
- **You have trouble completing a project because you think there is always something more you can do to make it better.** You obsess about sharing your book, project, meal, invitation, business card, website, article, or speech with others. You want to make sure your work is the best it can be before revealing it.
- **You use the word "should" a lot.** "I should do this," and "They should do that," may be common phrases, both out loud and inside your head. You have certain "rules" you believe that you, and others, should follow. And when those rules aren't followed, you are not pleased.
- **Your self-confidence depends on what you accomplish and how others react to you**. You strive for excellence and need validation from others to feel good about your accomplishments. What's more, once you have achieved a goal, you quickly move on to the next one.
- **You tend to fixate on something you messed up**. You may have done something right, but still focus instead on the one mistake you made.
- **You procrastinate, or avoid situations where you think you might not excel**. It may seem counterintuitive, but many people who procrastinate or avoid doing something are actually perfectionists: They're afraid they will fail. Their rationale is, "I might not be able to do it perfectly, so why bother at all?" https://www.psychologytoday.com/us/blog/better-perfect/201611/9-signs-you-might-be-perfectionist

9. ☐ **Indecisiveness** – When we are faced with more than one option, we are unable to choose an option and run with it. We spend excessive time going over the options without coming to a conclusion. Yet again, this can be traced back to poorly defined

goals. When we have clearly defined goals, we have clear criteria for determining the most important thing that we can do at any given moment in time. We determine which task/project is going to get our time based on the return that we will receive from completing that task.

Often people can't let go of an option because it feels limiting. If they say "no," to an option, then they are taking that possibility off the table. If we can only choose one course of action, every other option must be eliminated. With clear goals we can cross off options that don't propel our decision toward that goal. It isn't uncommon for people to have loose goals, or no goals which then opens up the possibility of multiple options and can cause indecisiveness.

Look at the projects and tasks you are to perform. Label them 1-5 as the top priority. Leave the other 20 items alone. They will be there. Don't let them distract you from 1, then 2, then 3, then 4, and so on.

Poorly Defined Goals and Indecisiveness

I worked with a group of leaders about identifying some issues that may be causing confusion, disorientation from the mission and lack of progress. It was based on an employee survey. I followed up with division leaders in the company to get their take on what may be casuing the low employee satisfaction scores.

After much deliberation, discussion and sorting the issues into three main categories, I concluded that they had three issues to address. 1. Lack of Leadership Alignment – they all were doing their own things without a unifying leader to bring it all together. They floated. 2. Poor Communication – they often failed to identify what needed communicated, why it needed communicated and how to properly communicate the correct information. 3. Too Many Initiatives.

It was the third issue, that would provide the greatest impact on the way they were perceived as leaders. I grabbed the dry-erase marker and stood with my back to them. I said, "Start shouting out the initiatives you all are working on." They did, and they continued to shout them out until I asked them to stop at 25 initiatives.

I stepped back from the whiteboard. Many of the initiatives were contingent on other initiatives to be completed before they were even viable. Many were low level and were being worked on prior to other initiatives that needed to occur first. I asked them, "How many of these initiatives are contingent on other initiatives being completed and implemented to even become relevent?" It stopped them in their tracks. They began to see that their brains were being clogged and dilluted by items that should not be taking up space because they were so low on the prioroty list. Yet, when I asked them, all of these were presented as if they were equally important.

I explained to them that about 20 of the initiatives should be tabled. Put them aside and come back to them when the timing is right, once you've implemented and established the top initiatives as the way we do business. We needed to make them the standard before we lump other initiatives on top of ungrounded change that has not take root. Simplify. This is an example of, "Look at all the work we have, and are working on, but not accomplishing anything for the long term." They couldn't decide or refused to decide which initiatives were priorities and therefore everything was a priority, which really meant, nothing was a priority. Goals and direction, clarify priorities.

Without clarity it's like telling someone to go to California. They may ask how should I do this and you simply reply, "Go West!" This doesn't take into consideration the timeframe, northern or southern California, cost to get there or why we are going.

"Don't interpret anything too much. This is time waster number 1." Dee Dee Artner

What is the most important task I can complete with the time and resources avialable to me?

10. ☐ **Saying "Yes" to Everything** – We want to operate from a place of assertiveness. Saying "no" all the time, could be seen as aggressive. Saying "Yes" to everything could be seen as a passive. The proper response to every question requires deliberation to

determine if what is being asked of us is doable. Can I fit it in? Do I have the time? If I don't, it is better to say, "I'd be happy to look at this in a month. Right now, I wouldn't want to take it on and not be able to work on it."

It is great to be able to help others, but if we are always helping others, we are rarely working on tasks which are important to us. Constantly saying "Yes" will leave us with an excessive workload. One of the quickest ways to improve our time management is to be assertive and learn to say "No."

From a work perspective, it can seem like a great idea to help others out and, it often is. But it is only helping them out if it is an ocassional occurrence. If we constantly do some of their work, we are not helping them out; we are doing their job for them. If they can't do their own work without having to constantly seek our help, then they have their own time management problems which need to be dealt with. We are enabling them to lower the bar.

By saying "yes" to every one of their requests, we are only helping them to avoid dealing with their poor time management and; we are damaging our own time management process.

*"The biggest difference between highly successful people
and the average person is that highly successful people
say, 'No' far more often."* (Warren Buffet)

11. ☐ **Doing Everything Yourself** – One of the clearest signs of poor time management is when we do everything ourself. It doesn't matter whether we are self-employed or an employee; there are always tasks which can be delegated, automated or outsourced. These tasks need to be identified and removed from our workload.

Quite often, we don't realize how much we do until disaster strikes and we spring straight into action. It may then cross our mind that we shouldn't be doing this, but we didn't even stop to think about whether it was a job for somebody else.

Maybe we are worried that others can't manage without us or, we feel that we must constantly prove our worth. Whatever the reasons, this is an unhealthy mindset and it will impact our physical health too, if it continues unchecked. Refer back to Empowerment in Chapter 4 – Motivation for more ideas on delegating.

Excellent Time Management is not defined by the amount of work we do or, how important we are deemed to be. An endless task list is more often a sign of poor time managmenet than good. A good time manager makes use of all the resources at his/her disposal, including people, at any given time.

They understand the difference between being responsible for getting the work done and doing the work themselves. As soon as a task arrives on their desk, they can quickly determine if it is a job for somebeody else and if it is, they quickly move it on. What's more, they realize that delegation provides a great learning opportunity for the person whom they delegated to.

We can't make up for lost time, we can only do better in the future.

Just because I am responsible for getting something done doesn't mean that it has to be me who does it – trust, delegate and empower.

If you are a good time manager, you should have down time to think, clear your head and realign priorities. You should be able to complete the tasks you are responsible for and then partake in true relaxation. True relaxation means not anxiously waiting for your next task, or sitting quietly thinking about your next task. It means not thinking about anything other than what YOU want to think about. It means clearing your head and resting to prepare your energy levels and attitude for the next big challenge. Everyone needs time with themselves without distractions to rejuvenate and center themselves. If this isn't happening in your life start now and figure this out. The video below will help focus your perspective as it relates to time and the "elasticity of time." Remember, Parkinson's Law as we'll discuss in the next chapter states – the activity will fit into the time allotted for it.

Improving Time Management Skills

Video – Laura Vanderkam – Gain Control of Your Free Time
https://www.ted.com/talks/laura_vanderkam_how_to_gain_control_of_your_free_time

"There are 168 hours in each week. How do we find time for what matters most? Time management expert Laura Vanderkam studies how busy people spend their lives, and she's discovered that many of us drastically overestimate our commitments each week, while underestimating the time we have to ourselves." (Ted.com)

10 Tips to Improve your Time Management Skills

1. **Delegate** – part of being a leader is understanding what skill sets people have, how they work, and what work they like to perform. Delegating a task isn't pushing it on someone else it's expressing and demonstrating that you trust them to do something you find valuable.

Additional Tips for Delegation

1. **Learn to let go** – contrary to what many of us believe – others can do it just as well as us.
2. **Establish a firm priority system** – example of priority system is below.
3. **Focus on the strengths of the people we delegate to** – set others up for success.
4. **Provide instructions and clarity** – what does good look like?
5. **Teach new skills when necessary** – it's our job as leaders to help people grow and develop.
6. **Trust but Verify** – give them room to succeed, but stay close in case they need guidance and to ensure it is moving along.
7. **Communicate Openly** – be ready to tell somone great job, also be ready to correct what they've done. Ask them how the process

could have gone better and be ready to give them what they need.

2. **Prioritize Work** – I'll bet when your boss sends an email, you open it up immediately. If you don't, you may want to reevaluate how you determine your priorities. Think in terms of what needs done now, and then start knocking them off the list. Don't be afraid to drop unnecessary or fruitless tasks.

	URGENT	NOT URGENT
IMPORTANT	DO IT NOW	PLAN IT
NOT IMPORTANT	DELEGATE	DROP IT

3. **Schedule Tasks** – if we schedule ourselves specifically for certain tasks, then we know we have that time set aside to perform them. We must be comfortable stopping one task and starting another even if that means we must ask someone to allow us to be left alone.

4. **Set up Deadlines** – deadlines act as beacons and constantly flash and remind us that an item is due. If there is no deadline, what is going to trigger us to pursue the task, and in fact, what makes it a priority if there isn't a deadline? Look at dropping it.

5. **Avoid Procrastination** – we procrastinate on the things we don't want to do. When, in reality, we should work just the opposite. Do what we like least, first, so we can focus on other tasks with our full attention. If something is hanging over our head because we've procrastinated, our brain will not fire on all cylinders and will be distracted by the lingering deadline. Guilt may even invade us and further derail our efforts.

6. **Avoid Stress** – one way to minimize stress is to not procrastinate. But further, avoid people and situations that cause our demeanor and attitude to suffer or cause a negative mindset.

7. **Avoid Multitasking** – "Research conducted by Stanford University found that multitasking is less productive than doing a single thing at a time. The researchers also found that people who are regularly bombarded with several streams of electronic information cannot pay attention, recall information, or switch from one job to another as well as those who complete one task at a time." (Forbes.com)

"Another study conducted by the University of London found that people who multitasked during cognitive tasks experienced IQ score declines that were similar to what they'd expect if they had smoked marijuana or stayed up all night. IQ drops of 15 points for multi-tasking men lowered their scores to the average range for an 8 year old child." (Forbes.com)

8. **Start Early** – No time like the present. To truly have free-time, we must have nothing pressing to do. Get tasks done early, revise the result, review it, and then take some time to relax, recharge and not think about things that we should be doing…because, they are already complete.

9. **Take Regular Breaks** – "Employees need a sufficient amount of both motivation and ability to perform at their full potential (Meijman & Mulder, 2013). Work tasks are demanding. They require employees to resist distractions and persist on work goals for extended periods of time (Muraven, Tice, & Baumeister, 1998). For example, during tedious tasks, the average employee's ability to focus and persist on the job gets harder by the minute (Jung et al., 1997)." (Psychologytoday.com)

10. **Learn to say "No."** – Practice being assertive and try to operate *in the Infinite Space between* passive and aggressive behavior. Say what you mean and mean what you say. No is ok. It's better than saying "yes," and failing or driving yourself to a nervous breakdown. Again, to quote Warren Buffet,

"The biggest difference between highly successful people and the average person is that highly successful people say, 'No' far more often."

Time Management is often the difference between running our lives and our lives running us. Time management is about control. It's about understanding that time is a resource just like money and that when we allow ourselves to waste our time, or we allow others to waste our time, we are actually allowing someone to steal from us. We can make more money, but we can't make more time. All we can do is use the time we have, better. We should do with our time what we want for the maximum personal and professional benefit. That benefit may be that we do a great job, finish our work on time and keep our job, or it may be that we manage our time well and are able to sit quietly, worry free each day for an hour or spend an hour focusing our complete attention on our family.

Whatever we value in life, time is necessary for us to enjoy it. Manage our time so we can manage our lives and the satisfaction we receive. We wouldn't throw money away, don't throw our time away either.

CHAPTER 8

✦ ✦ ✦ CHAPTER 8 ✦ ✦ ✦

CALLING, AND CONDUCTING PRODUCTIVE MEETINGS

ACCORDING TO RESEARCH FROM THE Harvard Business School and the London School of Economics,

"Executives spend 18+ hours per week in meetings with an estimated 25-50% of meeting time considered wasted."

A Brief Introduction

Meetings can either propel our day and inspire us, or drag our day into the depths of dissatisfaction and frustration. We've all attended meetings that we dread to walk into and can't wait to leave. Just like we've all been attendees at meetings that we can't wait for and wish they never would end. We've also wondered, "What the hell are we even trying to accomplish here?"

A good leader knows when a meeting is necessary and when it will be productive but also knows when it is not appropriate to meet and a waste of time. Research done in 2012 by Salary.com indicates that 47% of people see meetings as a time waster. Professionals estimate that they lose 31 hours a month on unproductive meetings. (CBS News) It is also reported that 73% of people who attend meetings do other work during the meetings. (Wolf Management Consultants)

Let's start with the assumption that no one wants to sit in a meeting where their time is wasted and they have no idea what the point is. That figuratively and literally, sounds like hell. **Parkinson's Law** in project management states that work expands so as to fill the time available for its completion. Conversely then, it would make sense that we are able to do more work in less time, if the timeframe required it.

Parkinson's Law

My sons (soon to be 16 and 17) and I have always built things together, worked together outside and often ended up with one of us mad afterward. Usually it boils down to one of them being difficult with the other one. I'm very careful to explain to them what we are going to do, how we are going to do it and who's doing what. This often has no bearing on the outcome of the situation. What seems to be more of a factor is whether or not they are interested or have something else they want to do.

The starkest example was recently when a giant pair of oak trees, joined at the base, each roughly 36 inches in diameter, fell under the weight of an early November ice storm. The leaves hadn't fallen off yet and they collected an immense amount of ice which split the base down the middle. Each tree fell 180 degrees away from the other. One fell across the creek and the other fell into our driveway and blocked the entrance to the garages. It was Saturday and I worked on the trees all morning while my sons were at wrestling practice. I broke it down into manageable pieces and looked forward to their help moving the larger logs into piles.

They pulled in with my wife, (their mom) and I could see it in their faces; they were whooped from wrestling practice. They moseyed up the driveway, through the downed tree limbs like cowboys after a long cattle drive and were clearly uninterested in doing anything with the tree. They glanced at me like I was a stranger on the side of the road. I said, "Guys, go inside and get changed. I need you to come out and help me so we can get this tree out of our way." My youngest son, Jude, said, "I was going to Liv's house." I said, "You can after we get this taken care of. It won't take long." My older son, Hayduke, had nothing to do and said that his back was sore. Jude came out of the house in a couple minutes and we began to move the logs. My older son, who heard the conversation about Jude going to Alivia's came out about ten minutes later. Usually it was Jude who dragged his feet on jobs like this, but this time due to the unlimited amount of time Duke had that afternoon, he was in no hurry. Jude muttered under his breath, "What is Duke doing? What's taking him so long?"

Duke came out and Jude said, "Let's go, I want to get this done so I can go over to Liv's." Duke, was in no hurry, but if he had plans you can imagine he would have been a workhorse and hauled, pulled, carried and moved the logs like he usually did. At one point, Jude even said, "Come on, stop standing around," which was what Duke usually said to his little brother, Jude.

The roles were reversed that day due to the amount of time available to perform the task at hand for each of them. Efficiency isn't just a matter of motivation, it is also a matter of time. But time and the amount of time available obviously can be a powerful motivator. You can generally expect that the amount of time set aside for a project will likely be the amount of time it takes to perform the work, and a meeting is no different.

Duke would have been content dragging his feet on this project all afternoon because he had the time and nothing else to do. Where Jude had planned to make a quick turnaround and head out immediately after getting home, had little time. Duke valued his time much less than Jude valued his in that instance. Jude worked circles around Duke that day when most often it would have been the opposite.

I am also not ignorant to the fact that the big brother saw and took an amazing opportunity to balance the scale and put the equity theory to work for all the times his little brother slacked off when the three of us worked on projects because he had nothing better to do. If people don't have the time, they will not be productive and will likely be bitter if a meeting is held that isn't necessary or if people perceive that their time could be spent better, elsewhere.

Often meetings operate the same way. We spend as much time as the meeting is set for to accomplish the task at hand when in reality it could have been done much faster, and better, if people were motivated toward an outcome. Often, meetings begin without a clear purpose, agenda, or timeframe and end with little to no actionable items or decisions. It's similar to a meeting – if the organizer has time, a meeting isn't a big deal, (to them) but often the people who are invited to participate don't have the time, so they are distracted, unless the meeting is important to the participants and helps them do their job better. If it doesn't, this is death to morale. The problem my boys ran into was that they had inconsistent ideas about the acceptable timeframe to accomplish the goal.

Consider what I could have done better to get them both on the same page with the meeting/project/goal?

People will take 8 hours to do 4 hours of work if the timeframe to accomplish the task allows it.

There are many factors involved when the idea to hold a meeting comes to mind. Who, where, what's the goal/outcome we are working toward, and how long will it take to accomplish this outcome. As a rule of thumb, before we get too deep into the proper way to execute a meeting, let's ask ourselves a few questions.

What is the Purpose of the Meeting?

If the answer to this question is not explicitly clear, think real hard about whether or not you want to ask a group of people to come to a room and watch you flounder.

Should We Even Meet?

Before a meeting actually takes root on an Outlook calendar, be sure that it is necessary. We need to evaluate the situation, and decide whether alternate approaches to accomplish the goal are available. Which means first, we must have a goal. There must be something to accomplish. If there is not a clear goal, define one, or don't meet. Is there another appropriate venue to accomplish the same outcome without meeting? Will an email suffice? Will a quick conversation be adequate? Will a presentation communicate the message?

What is the Appropriate Timeframe to Meet?

> *With the average attention span down from 12 seconds in the year 2000 to 8 seconds in 2018, we don't even have the attention span of a goldfish, which is on average 9 seconds.*

A general rule as to what the appropriate timeframe to meet is; as short as possible. Get in, discuss, take action, conclude and get out.

Who Should Attend the Meeting?

Stakeholders, decision makers, people who may be affected by the decision, and experts are the most common cast of attendees. Don't waste someone's time inviting them because you're afraid you may hurt their feelings. Just talk to them and clear the air. Explain that you are simply being respectful of their time.

Meeting Preparation Checklist Prior to Calling a Meeting

Harvard Business Publishing (HBR.Org), Running Meetings – The Twenty Minute Manager Series has developed a Meeting Preparation Checklist to assist in running meetings. The checklist is simple and straight forward but will also provide you with decision points as to whether or not the meeting is actually necessary.

☐ **Identify the purpose of the meeting** – if it's unclear, regroup or don't call the meeting.

☐ **Make sure you really need a meeting** – see above.

☐ **Develop a preliminary agenda** – This will focus your thoughts and allow for timeframe adjustments.

☐ **Select the right participants and assigned roles** – Identify who *needs* to be there.

☐ **Decide where and when to hold the meeting** – ensure space and tech are adequate.

☐ **Confirm availability of the space** – schedule and reserve the space needed.

☐ **Send the invitation** – give enough time for people to plan or rearrange their calendars if necessary.

☐ **Send the preliminary agenda** - this plants the seed and gets everyone thinking about the topics the meeting will cover.

☐ **Send pre-reading or requests which require advance preparation** – well in advance so people can come prepared and not waste time.

☐ **Follow up with invitees in person, if appropriate** – if one person in particular is critical, make sure they can commit to being there.

☐ **Choose the decision making process that will be used** - majority vote, group consensus, or leader's choice.

☐ **Identify, arrange for, and test any required equipment** – arrive early and test and give yourself time to work out any kinks.

☐ **Finalize the agenda and distribute it to all participants** – provides expectations and keeps people focused and on task.

☐ **Verify that all key participants will attend and know their roles** – this can occur face-to-face or in a follow-up email.

☐ **Prepare yourself** - draft presentations, printed handouts, etc.

Meeting Ground Rules

It is completely acceptable to establish ground rules for meetings and in fact it is highly recommended. Many times ground rules revolve around respect, courtesy and how meeting decisions will be made. People will appreciate the candor and expectations. It is always a good idea to get everyone on the same page with expectations prior to beginning any endeavor. Some examples are:

Expectations of the Meeting Chairperson – (Make sure everyone knows you are the chairperson and then act like it.)

- **Make the Objectives Clear** – are we problem solving, sharing information, making decisions, or seeking input from experts to overcome an issue.

Objectives are goals, and people need to
know where they are trying to go,
so they can work efficiently to get there and feel good once they arrive.

- **Stick to Your Schedule (agenda)** – when people know what to expect, and can prepare and contribute based on those expectations, meetings become more valuable.
- **Avoid Monopolization of the Meeting** - It isn't uncommon for one member to have a greater stake in the content of the meeting. These people will often monopolize the meeting with their comments at the detriment of the group and the process. The person running the meeting should publicly redirect the conversation back to the group when this happens. This sets the tone for the group and alerts everyone that we are a collective, not individuals. It may be valuable to state, "Thank you for your comments, however, we also need to hear from others. "John, what are your thoughts on the topic?" We do not want to interrupt, or talk over other members as this becomes anarchistic and unproductive. The

meeting Chairperson (the person who called the meeting) must manage this.

- **Begin and End on Time** – if people aren't in the room at the time the meeting is to begin, start without them. They won't be late next time and it sets the stage for future meetings and the accountability to arrive and start on time. End on time – it is respectful to everyone in the meeting that their time is valued and expectations are met. Otherwise, expect people to get up and walk out because they are responsible for their time and the next item to attend to.

- **Ban Technology** – make it clear that cell-phones, i-pads, computers are not welcome in the meeting unless absolutely necessary. These are distractions from the discussion and the task at hand. As good as people say or think they are at multi-tasking, "It has been scientifically demonstrated that the brain cannot effectively or efficiently switch between tasks, so you lose time. It takes four times longer to recognize new things so you're not saving time; multitasking actually costs time. You also lose time because you often make mistakes. (Forbes.com)

If the message you want to send to everyone in the meeting is that you don't care, are uninterested and/or that what you are doing on that little hand held device is more important than what is happening right in front of you, with actual people, keep looking down at it and continue to alienate the people around you. Your call. It's your rep.

- **Follow-up** – send minutes with the facts, decisions and outcomes. The follow-up should also include who is responsible for taking action as a result of the meeting and any deadlines associated with decisions. This is a very critical component to meetings.

Accountability is critical to meeting success and people like to know what is expected of them. People want to do good work, contribute and be successful. Set the framework for them to feel good about contributing and meeting your expectations.

Expectations of Meeting Participants

- **Arrive on Time** – If participants are late, they should fully expect the meeting to already be underway. Remember from Communication, Chapter 3 that the message you're sending to everyone in the room is:

You can wait. Don't you know my time is more important than yours... or worse, you are insignificant?

- **Keep an Open Mind** – Progress is easier when people are open to other ideas, especially ideas that may not have been considered in the past. It is also advisable to be ready to let your ideas go if the group isn't taking the bait and picking up what you are laying down.

  The goal isn't to be right, the goal is to collaborate and find the best answer to the issue at hand.

  Leaders don't need to have all the answers they just need to be able to solicit the right answer from the right people and know when they hear it.

- **Listen to the Opinions of Others** – If you want to be heard when you have something to say, listen to others when they speak. It's the principle of reciprocity in action.

  The longer one listens attentively, the more power their words have when they speak.

- **Participate** – Participants have been invited because it is believed that they have something to offer to the group. Don't let the group down. It's very similar to something I heard Larry

Bird and my former coach explain about shooting and your responsibility to the team. I'm paraphrasing, but;

If you're open, and no one has a better shot,
it's your job to shoot the basketball.
If you don't, you're letting your team down.

- **Avoid Monopolization** – if as a participant you feel like you're dominating the discussion, and the chairperson hasn't intervened, be respectful and stop...ask another person their opinion on the topic. Be honest and objective with yourself. Rewind the tape in your head. Are you doing all the talking?
- **Avoid Conflict Situations** – conflict is not necessarily a bad thing, ie, Margaret Heffernon's video *"Dare to Disagree"* from Chapter 5, however, if conflict is started for the sake of conflict, or "throwing darts" at people, refrain and try to be respectful in disagreements. But of course, never acquiesce to group think or poor decisions without expressing your viewpoint.
- **Side Conversations** – simply do not participate. It is a distraction, rude and unproductive. Save it for after the meeting.
- **Ask Questions to Clarify** – seek clarification, but do not ask questions to push someone into a corner or put them on their heels unless absolutely necessary. Be aware of fast talkers.

"Fast talkers say things faster than they can be assessed, as a way of pushing their agenda past other people's examination or objections. Fast talking can be especially effective when it's used against people worried about appearing stupid — don't be one of those people. Recognize that it's your responsibility to make sense of things, and don't move on until you do. If you're feeling pressured, say something like, "Sorry for being stupid, but I'm going to need to slow you down so I can make sense of what you're saying." Then, ask your questions. All of them." (Ted.com, Ideas)

- **Take Notes** - that are relevant to action items you are responsible to produce. Share them with the group.

Meeting Expectations

This document was sent to all committee members in advance of the first meeting and shortly after they agreed to be part of the initiative.

Human Resources Committee - Charter

Charter Statement
The HR Committee was created with the intent of having a two way conversation with all corners of the Group of Companies as it relates to the work environment, employee satisfaction and our collective ability to get better at this thing called, "work."

Committee Selection
The original HR Committee was selected because they either graduated from or were currently in the HGC-Leadership Academy, and because of my belief that these people had a desire to make their own and everyone else's work-life more satisfying.

Terms
Committee appointment will last for 6 months. There is no limit to the number of 6 month appointments you can serve, but you cannot serve two in a row.

Meeting Times and Dates
We will meet once a month for lunch (lunch will be provided) in the Armory Training Room. Meetings will begin at 11:30 a.m. and conclude at 1:00 p.m. We will meet on the 3rd Wednesday of each month.

Organization
Meeting minutes will be taken so we stay focused and do not lose sight of our goals. These minutes will be shared between each meeting. An agenda will be distributed prior to each meeting so Committee Members have a chance to add pressing items for discussion. The meeting will be chaired by the VP of Human Resources and Leadership Development.

We will submit blind votes on whether an initiative should or should not be pursued.

Membership

Once 6 months have been served on the committee, it is up to you to find your replacement. Please let the Committee Chair know of your selection so the replacement can be brought up to speed quickly.

Agreements

1. *We will be respectful toward one another – stay focused, no sidebar conversations, avoid distractions ie, phones, computers, i-pads.*
2. *We will work in the best interest of the most people.*
3. *We will be open and honest – even if it isn't popular – this is a safe space.*
4. *"We will not make assumptions, we will do our best, we will be impeccable with our words and we won't take things personally." – Miguel Ruiz – the Four Agreements*

This document provides expectations and reference for when people are not adhering to the agreed upon standards to be part of the committee. Everyone wants to be part of something special and important. These documents can give the entire process the gravity it needs to be taken seriously and keep people focused.

Reasons Why Meetings May be Ineffective

Now that we know some of the parameters to meeting success, we'll look at the reasons many meetings are a waste of time, fall flat and leave people feeling as if they have been robbed of time, attention and brainpower.

- **The meeting is unnecessary**, and revolves around discussion of trivial issues, thus wasting members' valuable time.
- **The meeting lacks a clarity of purpose**, i.e., the aims and objectives are not clearly defined.

If a clear goal is not evident, rethink having the meeting.

- **Inappropriate style of leadership**, i.e., the chairperson dominates and closes down or disregards other contributions.

Today's workforce is about collaboration, teams and mutual respect. It's often a combination of naivety, arrogance and insecurity that cause a leader to minimize others and emphasize their own point of view.

- **The chairperson exercises little control** and allows one or two members to dominate the proceedings.

Chairpersons must encourage all to participate, otherwise, there is no reason to have the non-contributors in the meeting.

- **The meeting is too large** thereby limiting the flow of discussion and preventing all members from being able to contribute.
- **Decisions emerge that are not truly representative** – this can occur when the wrong people are in attendance. The decisions must represent the attitudes of the greater group and not the motives of one or two individuals.

This can be intentional or unintentional. If it is intentional it's usually a tactic to avoid hearing counter points or dissention from the meeting organizer's agenda. Be courageous and point it out for the greater good of the group and organization, not to mention that's what leader's do.

Remember, courage is not the absence of fear, it is overcoming fear and acting in defiance of your fear.

- **Problems are talked about rather than talked through** – this can be overcome by the chairperson ensuring that once the issue is dealt out to the group and discussed, the focus turns to problem solving and decision making. Ideally the decision will be a consensus.

It's easy to wallow in the problem. Some people like it.
True leadership identifies the issue and immediately
works to put solutions in place.

- **Decisions are delayed or not acted upon** – avoid "analysis paralysis," which is when a person or group of people can't eliminate unfavorable paths in favor of narrowing the focus to a positive, productive decision.

Analysis paralysis is painful to watch. Some folks don't want
to select a course of action because to them selecting one
course of action eliminates all other courses of action,
which is like being put into a box with no windows. They feel trapped.
So instead of deciding, they don't decide and
avoid accountability and responsibility.

- **No clear-cut decisions are made** – it may not always be possible to conclude every meeting with a decision for every issue, but that should be the goal.

"When there is an exchange of ideas, it is important to end it by
stating the conclusions. If there is agreement, say it; if not, say
that. When further action has been decided, get those tasks on a
to-do list, assign people to do them, and specify due dates. Write
down your conclusions, working theories and to-do's in places
that will lead to their being used as foundations for continued
progress. To make sure this happens, assign someone to make sure
notes are taken and follow-through occurs." (Ted.com, Ideas)

- **Minutes are inaccurate** or seen as being manipulated by the chairperson or secretary for his/her own purposes.
- **The wrong people are present**, thus preventing the meeting from proceeding effectively, e.g., those present have to refer

back to another person and are therefore unable to comment effectively. (Skillsyouneed.com)

As a meeting organizer, you want the people who are invited to your meeting to see the invite and feel positive and optimistic that they are getting ready to make progress. The way we organize, set expectations, and conduct meetings is the difference between sending people on their way feeling inspired, productive and as if they are a valued contributor to the organizational mission. Or we can send them away deflated and even further behind their work load. It is *in the Infinite Space between* the decision to meet and the conclusion of the meeting that matters. An employee that has their time wasted will likely not be an employee for long. Remember, the Equity Theory from Chapter 4. The intent of any meeting is to solidify and energize people toward a common goal, make strong decisions and inform. If this isn't happening, rethink meeting and the structure of the meeting.

As leaders, it is in our hands to ensure our communication, our leadership style, our organizational skills and the expectations we set affect people positively and inspire them to meet their own and the organization's goals. It feels good when we accomplish our aims. We're best as leaders, when we help people be their best.

CHAPTER 9

SPEAKING IN PUBLIC, AND CAPTURING AN AUDIENCE

A Brief Introduction

I CAN'T BREATHE. I CAN'T do this. I can't stop sweating. I'll just call off today. I'll fake an illness. No, I'll fall down the steps. I'll just drop out of school. I guess I'll just quit and go on welfare. I could go on and on about the irrational thoughts and ideas that run through a person's head leading up to and then actually speaking in public. The one thing they all have in common is that they are natural. They are hardwired into us and they are, in modern day society, unrealistic.

I say modern day society because these reactions are left over from millennia of humans dealing with actual fight or flight and now freeze moments. Likely, if you fought you either reinforced your confidence and overcame the fear or learned to avoid the danger so not to die. If your ancestors ran in the face of danger, they 1. May have preserved the gene pool for future progeny, but also even more deeply ingrained the fear as legitimate. 2. If ancient people froze in the face of a giant Saber Toothed Tiger, the gene pool likely ended with them.

Public Speaking invokes the same response in modern people as an encounter with a Saber Toothed Tiger in our not so distant past. Parlay this into the modern workforce. If you can overcome your fear of speaking, you and your career are likely to flourish. If you avoid, or run from public speaking, you are only giving the irrational fear power by condoning it as a legitimate issue that must be avoided and your career becomes limited. To stay, fight and overcome your fear will result in decreased fear and more familiarity with the scary subject whether it is a Saber Toothed Tiger or just a bunch of people in a room waiting to hear what you have to say.

Courage is not the absence of fear,
it is overcoming fear and acting in defiance of it.

Overcoming Fear

I grew up performing in front of people from the time I was 5. I put all of my experience and practice on center stage nearly every week of my young, young adult, and early adult life from the time I was 5 -22. I was nervous until I was about 8. At 8 I began to receive positive reinforcement for my performances and began to look forward to that stage, with all eyes upon me, the cheers and the questions afterward. I am referring to sports; basketball, football and baseball. I would go out on a court or field right now, and have absolutely zero fear of failure or embarrassment. Why? I practiced. I practiced and played these sports (especially basketball) more than anything ever in my life, even to this day. I have confidence in my ability to perform. I'm 47.

What does this have to do with Public Speaking? Everything! Public speaking is a performance. You are the starring actor and your audience wants to be entertained. It's no different than sports or anything else that people come to watch and be entertained by. That is, if you want to be successful.

I stammered, stuttered and swallowed my tongue throughout my early public speaking life (you know that very perceptible moment when you try to say a word and the back of your throat swallows and sucks the word back down into the bowels of your body and instead of a word, a gulp noise comes out of your mouth – a wordless breath.) This went on through my undergrad studies.

It wasn't until I was in my first class in grad school – Sociology – that epiphany struck me. I had to stand in front of the class for 45 minutes and present on the racial inequities in the US – how it began, how it continued and why. I was terrified. The thing I had going for me was that I felt extremely strong about the subject. I shuffled to the podium in front of the class, shook, weak kneed, and sweated. I rambled down the path for 20 minutes – and mostly read from my cards. I tried to make controversial arguments, inflammatory claims and provocative comments. As time went on, I began to look at the audience for their reaction. Sometimes it happened and sometimes it didn't, but what I very clearly remember coming into clarity was, "No One Cared!" I continued on, but with a different self-assurance. It occurred to me also, that no one was really paying attention because they either just did what I was doing, or were likely scared to death of doing what I was doing in the near future, not to mention, I had given them no reason to care.

They certainly weren't judging me, but they certainly weren't hanging on every word. Afterward, when I ran the tape back in my head I also realized that I missed a terrific opportunity to make an impact. I had a class room full of people and their attention was on me, or should have been, but that was my fault it wasn't. I felt strongly about my topic and I missed an opportunity to affect all of these people in a positive way. I never made that mistake again.

I realized as I continued to be "forced" to speak in public throughout my career that I was not looking at public speaking through the right lens. "Forced!?" No! It was an opportunity and a gift. I had a captive audience and that audience was either going to absorb or ignore what I said. The only factor affecting that, was me.

Fast forward to present day, or at least December 6th, 2018, when I pulled the biggest stunt in any public speaking engagement I'd ever had. I was in Dallas, TX at a Construction HR conference. I was asked to be a speaker. My timeslot was the first day, right after lunch. I knew that timeslot would be tough. I also knew I had to hatch a plan to capture the audience's attention, keep it and send them on their way with a positive remembrance of their time with me. I tell people all the time who are nervous about speaking in public, "it doesn't really matter what you say, the audience is only going to remember about 10-15% or less. What you want to do is leave them in a place so that when they think back to the event, to you, they have a positive emotional reaction to the time they spent with you. Then, they are likely to remember more.

Earlier that day, the conference began with the MC making bold statements like, "Let's be courageous over cautious, and playful yet professional." I thought back to his comments as I brainstormed an attention grabbing introduction. There were 200 HR executives in the room – my kind of crowd. They were split roughly 50/50, men/women. The stage was about 30 feet wide with stairs that lead up on the left and right. From the main stage, a catwalk jetted into the audience about 20 feet. At the end of the catwalk was a monitor where the presenters spent most of their time. Behind the stage was a 20 foot wide projector screen. I had a microphone clipped to my lapel. I was hands free and there was no podium to hide behind, which was fine, because as you'll see, it's easier to connect with the audience.

I stood in the wings and the MC introduced me. I could feel my knees get a little weak, like I was about to get into a fight as a kid. My pits became moist but I had a jacket on, so no risk of sweat pod bleed through.

"Let's welcome Matt Hess. People clapped lazily. Many still looked at their smartphones to see what they'd missed at the office that morning. I moved toward the stage and as the very lackluster clapping died down, I hit the bottom step to the stage and began. "In light of Christian's (MC) earlier comments about being courageous over cautious and playful yet professional..." I hit the top of the stage and took a hard and flamboyant, right turn down the cat walk. I did my best (model on a runway walk,) and said, "Today, Matt's wearing a jacket by Chaps." I hit the end of the catwalk, unbuttoned my jacket, and whipped around and headed away from the audience and back down the cat walk. They giggled and laughed behind me. I continued, "His shirt, and pants are by Banana Republic. His boots, Allen Edmonds."

I turned and faced the audience with a giant smile on my face. The audience erupted and clapped, but most importantly, I had their attention. I said, "It's not very often I get a chance to walk the catwalk. I couldn't resist. I'm sure a lot of you can do that way better than me, but that's what I have." They sat up in their chairs and quite frankly, I believed they wanted to see where this was going to go and quite optimistically I believed they wanted to hear what I had to say. I think I intrigued them, but of course that was the point. I believed that no matter what happened from that point forward, for the next 20 minutes, I would have left them with a positive emotional remembrance of our time together. But, would I ever really know?

I went to the reception afterward for drinks and hors de' oeuvres. In line at the bar, for a pinot noir, two woman and man stood to the right. "Matt!" I looked. "We were just talking about you." I said, "Yes?" and skeptically smiled. They played it cool. "We were just talking about who was the best speaker." (Mind you, they did not say, we were talking about who had the best content.) I smiled. One of the woman said, "We loved you. That was so funny! We needed that after lunch." "Thanks. I'm really glad you enjoyed it," I said.

Other people throughout the evening walked toward me and did their best catwalk routine. I walked up to a group standing around a high top table to introduce myself. The man said, "I was just quoting you." Maybe, just maybe, they did listen to the content, but would they have if I hadn't pull that stunt? I don't know, but I knew I wasn't willing to take that chance.

I thought about it afterward, would that have worked if the room was filled with engineers - No? Would that have worked if the room was filled with Marketing or Business Development people – maybe… probably. Would it have worked if the room was filled with CEO's? Maybe…probably not. Would it have worked if it were all men? No! To be frank, I wasn't sure it was going to work with the audience I knew best – a bunch of HR nerds - but that was the inherent anxiety we all feel in those situations, but it is not grounded in reality.

We have to know our audience, we have to know our limits, and we have to understand what we are trying to accomplish each time we stand in front of a room and address a crowd. The opening lines that helped put the idea into perspective and hatch the plan in the first place were key. It also turned out to be excellent advice for anyone expected to speak in public. Don't forget…

Be Courageous over Cautious. Be Playful, yet Professional.
Authenticity is what people want, not a canned,
contrived dissemination of information.

VIDEO - Mikael Cho – Talks about The science of stage fright (and how to overcome it) in his Ted Talk below.
<u>**https://www.ted.com/talks/mikael cho the science of stage fright and how to overcome it**</u>

People experience fear and anxiety in what many surveys say, is the thing people are afraid of most – even more than death. How could this be? Well, in death, you feel nothing. In public speaking, you feel out of control, it is painful and your body reacts in a way that is extremely uncomfortable and even contributes to another major human fear, the fear of failure. Let's get this out of the way so we can understand that this fear isn't a weakness in us, it is a natural occurrence and it can be overcome.

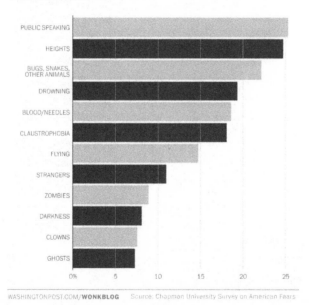

What are you so afraid of?

% of Americans who say they fear...

WASHINGTONPOST.COM/**WONKBLOG**   Source: Chapman University Survey on American Fears

The Book of Lists reports the Top Ten Human Fears as:

1.	**Speaking before a Group**	6.	**Death**
2.	Heights	7.	Flying

3. Financial problems
4. Deep water
5. Sickness

8. Loneliness
9. Dogs

*"I guess we'd rather be in the casket than
delivering the eulogy." (Jay Leno)*

Practice Equals Comfort

*I worked as a carpenter's apprentice in the summers and on breaks from
college. An 8:12 pitched roof is pretty steep at roughly 39 degrees. It's about
like this. The first time I stepped onto a roof at that angle, I knelt down to
lower my center of gravity and climbed to the crest of the roof, basically
on all fours. I treated it like I was climbing a rock wall - always have three
points of contact on the rock. I asked the foreman, "What do you do if you
fall and start to slide?" He sort of looked at me like I was an idiot, but he said
anyway, "Pull your hammer out and jam the claw through the plywood to
stop yourself." That sounded like, "Go get the board stretcher," to me. Total
B.S. I watched the guys I worked with walk horizontal, diagonal and vertical
like Spiderman. To me, it looked like they carried plywood, threw it down
into place and hammered it home without the height or fear of falling two
stories anywhere near the surface of their psyche.*

*That first day, I practiced three points of contact. I knelt and
hammered down plywood and scooted on my butt. That first Monday
bled into Tuesday and so on through the week. I spent the entire week on
that roof. By the end of the day Friday I was able to have run if I wanted to.*

*Public speaking is no different. In fact, it's almost exactly the same.
I had to gain confidence through repetition and familiarity until finally,
walking on a steep roof and carrying full sheets of plywood was no different
than walking on flat land. Public speaking can be the same as having a
one-on-one conversation if we become familiar and confident and are able
to reframe the experience to find opportunity and value.*

*"Fear creates anger, anger creates hatred and
hatred creates suffering." (Yoda)*

Just like

Repetition creates familiarity, familiarity creates confidence and confidence creates success.

The question we have to ask ourselves is, "Are our careers going to be debilitated and stunted because we're afraid, or are we going to stare fear in the face, realize it's irrational, and conquer it?" No one has ever died from public speaking. I mean, it's not a Saber Toothed Tiger.

Parts of a Speech

Every public speech or address falls into one of 3 general categories. We'll look at those later. And each speech is segmented into three very simple parts. The parts of the speech outlined below are from: (speechanddebate.rog)

1. **The Introduction** – is intended to develop rapport with the audience. This can be accomplished through an <u>attention grabbing</u> statistic, narrative, story or quote. You are also trying to find <u>common ground</u> with your audience. The audience needs to feel that you are one of them or at least an expert that should be listened to. They need to know that you know what you are talking about but through their lens of reality. <u>The thesis</u> is what you are going to focus on. It is what your speech is trying to convey. You want to <u>preview</u> the information to come and set the stage for the audience to either be informed, persuaded or have something demonstrated to them.

2. **Body** – the body of your speech is where you'll either share, convince or inform your audience. It is where you discuss the <u>problem, or reason</u> you are speaking at all. You'll provide supporting evidence to your claim or angle and share this in a logical and meaningful way. You'll employ <u>transition</u> techniques which we'll discuss below. You'll discuss the <u>causes</u> of the problem or the symptoms that have brought the issue to light and ideally appeal to the audience's logic by

presenting examples and evidence. You'll transition to the <u>solutions</u> to the problem you're talking about.

3. **Conclusion** – the conclusion is short, and should <u>summarize the problem</u> and the <u>solution</u> succinctly. You'll want to <u>restate your thesis</u> and <u>give a final statement</u>. Whatever you do to close your speech, please, please, please do not say things like, "Well," shrug your shoulders, "That's all I have." End with a bang! Make sure the last words the audience hears from you are good ones. You want them to walk away having a positive remembrance of your time together.

Tell them what you are going to say, say it,
and then tell them what you said.

3 General Types of Speeches

1. **Informative Speeches** – an informative speech is necessary when there is a void of knowledge and you are charged with filling that void through your speech. This could be on any topic from National Security to How to Change your Oil.

Informative Speech Tips – Writing and Presenting

A. **Capture the audience's** attention and hold it. It doesn't matter what the content of your presentation is, or how much people need the information if the speaker can't engage the audience and capture their attention. First, capture the audience then release the information. We'll discuss in greater detail how to capture an audience further in the chapter.

B. **Include as much information** as possible in the speech without overshadowing the original point or topic. Often people try to include so much information that the point, or message is lost. The key is to whittle the content down for maximum effectiveness.

C. **Research, research, and then reference!!** Be sure to research your topic. If you are going to inform people on a topic, you should be up to speed with all the relevant information regarding it.

D. **Stay on track** to keep the audience focused. This circles back to the information you choose to present. Make sure that what you choose to share pushes the knowledge and understanding of the audience, rather than confuse them.

E. **Catch spelling, grammar, and punctuation errors** to ensure you repeat everything correctly while giving the speech. If you write it wrong in your speech, you'll say it wrong. You want your speech to have no unnecessary obstacles, like you stumbling over punctuation or putting the wrong emphasis on the wrong part of the sentence.

F. **Have proper transitions** in the speech to bring the audience from one idea to the next, fluently. We've all sat in a presentation and wondered, "What just happened? What are we talking about now?" Generally, it is because the speaker didn't transition between topics smoothly or logically.

   When you are transitioning between points/topics or ideas consider using the below words to clarify what is happening for the audience when transitioning from;

   1. **Similar Topics or Points**, you can use words like; Likewise, Similarly, This is just like, or, We see the same thing if we consider"

   2. **Contrasting Points**, words like; Conversely, On the contrary, If we flip that around, The opposing argument, Yet, we cannot ignore...

   3. **To Elaborate on an Idea**, use words like; Also, Moreover, In addition, Furthermore

   4. **Numbered Ideas or Points,** use words like First, or the First step is, and so on.

   5. **Cause and Effect Relationships**, use words like; Therefore, As a Result, Consequently.

6. **Transition from Introduction to the Body of the Speech**, use words like; Let's begin by looking at, Now that we've given an overview, let's start with.

7. **Transition from Speech Body to Conclusion**, use words like; In Short, In Summary, or In Conclusion. (sixminutes. dlugan.com)

G. **Edit the speech** as much as needed after it is fully written. Do not edit the speech while writing it. You don't want unnecessary words, phrasings, examples or topics littered throughout your speech. The editing process is intended to narrow down the focus of the speech.

Writing a speech is like a band that gets together to jam. The drummer lays down a beat, the bass player adds a riff/ rhythm to the beat and the guitar player comes in and adds the melody. The singer begins to spout words. Write freely, riff like musicians and create with reckless abandon. Edit later.

H. **Include quotes and interesting facts** throughout the speech and at the end as well. If you've hooked the audience at the beginning, these can reinvigorate the audience's focus and attention.

I. **Avoid plagiarism** at all costs.

J. **Repeat things** that are main points to help the audience remember.

K. **Use guide phrases** such as; first, second, finally, then, I want you to remember…

2. **Demonstrative Speeches** – the point of a demonstrative speech is to illustrate through your words and actions how to perform some action or process. When developing a demonstrative speech it is important to follow a few guidelines. Demonstrative speeches lend themselves nicely to props and visuals. Be sure the props are relevant and clearly demonstrate the process you are sharing. Generally, these are the easiest speeches to prepare and present.

Demonstrative Speech Outline

Oddly, there is y to prepare, write and deliver a demonstrative speech. There is however, a basic speech outline to follow below.

A. **Start with Why** – Tell them why they need to know how to do what you are showing them. Why do they care?

B. **Give a Brief Overview of the Entire Process** – Give them a visual on where you are taking them so they can have a broad overview of what to expect the end result to be in their mind so they can create it in their mind and work through the process as you speak.

C. **Go through the Steps, One-by-One** – This is essentially the body or core of your presentation. This is the meat. Keep the steps as simple as possible. You must explain the purpose of the step and why it is there and cannot be skipped. If it can be skipped, skip it.

D. **Allow time for Questions** – This stage can reinforce what you've just demonstrated to the audience because if one person has a question, it is likely others do to. This part of the process can also provide insight into where you were not clear and what can be changed in your speech for next time.

E. **Summarize Briefly** – remember, anytime you are speaking in public it is always a good idea to tell them what you are going to say, say it, and then tell them what you said.

3. **Persuasive** –a persuasive speech is intended to conjure change in the audience's behavior or attitude toward a topic. It was nearly 2300 years ago that Aristotle described the 3 secrets to being a persuasive speaker. Amazingly, these principles still hold true today.

A. **Ethos** – refers to the level of credibility your audience perceives in you. It is their confidence in you that matters, not whether or not you are confident in yourself, but that does help. Do you have their respect? If not, how can you attain credibility with your audience?

Ethos can be gained by how <u>trustworthy</u> you appear to the audience. <u>Similarity</u> to the audience can increase Ethos. Find what you and the audience have in common and seek common ground. Are you an <u>Authority</u> on the topic? If so, don't be afraid to share with the audience in your introduction why you are an authority or expert or why they should even listen to you over someone else. It could be your passion, your experience, your education or some divine insight that you believe you have. Do you have a <u>reputation</u> for being an expert in the field? If so, share this. If it is very well accepted that you are an expert, then let your reputation precede you and dive into the topic. Don't be afraid to be the expert.

B. **Pathos** – refers to your ability to appeal to the emotions of the audience. You want the language you use to invoke the correct expression of love, sympathy, compassion, hate, contempt or fear for what you are saying. Emotionally charged stories are an excellent way to spark emotions and connectedness from people. Refer to: <u>http://sixminutes.dlugan.com/pathos-examples-speaking/</u> for 18 terrific tips to create an emotional connection with your audience. Some of the best tips are below.

Improving Pathos in Speeches

1. **Select Emotional Themes and Points** – just as I have taken a few selected tips from the above resource that I believe to be most impactful, make sure you choose the most effective points to make. Not all points are necessary or equal, but the right themes are critical.

2. **Choose words that add Emotional Emphasis** – some words are neutral and do not invoke an emotional response. Choose charged words that tickle the emotions you are want to stir up.

3. **Use Rich Analogies and Metaphors** – people relate their own experiences to yours through analogy and metaphor.

Because of this, an emotional response is shared between you and the audience.

4. **Tell Stories** – Storytelling is the oldest form of human dissemination of information. We are primed and ready to hear a great story – always, so tell one.

"Stories are often the quickest path to the greatest emotional connection with your audience." (Andrew Dlugan)

5. **Use Humor** – humor provides a deep sense of connection between people. If your audience is laughing, they are engaged and having fun.
6. **Be Authentic** – to share an emotion, you also have to feel it. If you aren't feeling the emotion you want them to feel, they will not feel it either. You will be a bad actor in B-movie if you are not authentic and committed.

C. **Logos** – is synonymous with, a logical argument. A logical argument must be made in conjunction with the emotional appeal of your speech. If it doesn't make sense, no matter how emotionally charged or compelling it is, the message will fall flat.

Improving Logos in Speeches

1. **Make it Understandable** – Is the audience able to understand the vocabulary you use? Are they absorbing the main points the way you want them to?
2. **Make it Logical** – Do your arguments make sense? Are you connecting the dots for the audience in a way that most of them can understand?
3. **Make it Real** – when possible use concrete and specific language. Use specific examples and stories over abstract and generalized ones.

Together Ethos, Pathos and Logos are the *persuasive appeals.* If you want your audience to be receptive to your persuasion, all three of these must be in-tact.

*"People buy on emotion (pathos) and justify
with fact (logos)."* (Bert Decker)

Is Ethos, Pathos or Logos most important in Persuasive Speeches?

*"Aristotle believed that logos should be the most important of the
three persuasive appeals. As a philosopher and a master of logical
reasoning, he believed that logos should be the only required persuasive
appeal. That is, if you demonstrated logos, you should not need either
ethos or pathos. However, Aristotle stated that logos alone is not
sufficient. Not only is it not sufficient on its own, but it is no more
important than either of the two other pillars. He argued that all three
persuasive appeals are necessary."* (Dulgan, Andrew, Six Minutes)

10 Public Speaking Tips

You've decided what type of presentation you are putting together to share with your audience. Now, it's time to develop the presentation according to your audience, and prepare yourself for a successful performance. Remember, it doesn't matter how great the information is, if no one is listening.

The 10 Tips below are from the Harvard Extension School of Professional Development. Marjorie North is a consultant for political candidates, physicians and lawyers and was the Clinical Director in the Department of Speech, Language Pathology and Audiology at Northeastern University.

1. Nervousness is Normal – Practice and Prepare

All people feel some physiological reactions like pounding hearts and trembling hands. Do not associate these feelings with the sense that you will perform poorly or make a fool of yourself. Some nerves are good. The adrenaline rush that makes you sweat also makes you more alert and ready to give your best performance. The best way to overcome anxiety is to prepare, prepare, and prepare some more. Take the time to go over your notes several times. Once you have become comfortable with the material, practice – a lot. Videotape yourself, or get a friend to critique your performance.

Practice with the goal being to increase your confidence.
This will inevitably lead to improved authenticity which
will lead to the audience having a significantly more
favorable impression about you and your topic.

Practice leads to Confidence and Confidence leads to Authenticity.

A good way to practice is to speak out loud and in front of a mirror at the same volume you will present. You will begin to feel the flow of the information and the opportunities to enhance your inflection, tone of voice, and eliminate any unusual, or distracting body movements. Remember, 85% of a face-to-face message is communicated through non-verbal cues and communication. Refer to Chapter 3 – Effective Communication – for a refresher.

2. **Know your Audience**

Your Speech is About Them, Not You. Before you begin to craft your message, consider who the message is intended for. Learn as much about your listeners as you can. This will help you determine your choice of words, level of information, organizational pattern, and motivational statement.

Speak the language your audience knows.
Use examples they can relate to.
Understand their concerns, interests and aspirations.

3. **Organize Your Material in the Most Effective Manner to Attain Your Purpose**

Create the framework for your speech. Write down the topic, general purpose, specific purpose, central idea and main points. Make sure to grab the audience's attention in the first 30 seconds.

4. Watch for Audience Feedback and Adapt to It

Keep the focus on the audience. Gauge their reactions, adjust your message and stay flexible. Delivering a canned speech will guarantee that you lose the attention of, or confuse even the most devoted audiences.

5. Let Your Personality Come Through

Be yourself, don't become a talking head – in any type of communication. You will establish better credibility if your personality shines through, and your audience will trust what you have to say if they can see you as a real person. In today's business climate, authenticity is becoming more and more important.

People want to see a real person, doing real things so they can relate to that person on an emotional human level, not just as a professional talking head.

6. Use Humor, Tell Stories, and Use Effective Language

Inject a funny anecdote in your presentation, and you will certainly be more likely to grab your audience's attention. Audiences generally like a personal touch in a speech. A story can provide that. Tell something personal about you or your family. Allow the audience to relate to you as a real person.

7. Don't Read Unless You Have to - Work from an Outline

Reading from a script or slide fractures the interpersonal connection. By maintaining eye contact with the audience, you keep the focus on yourself and your message. A brief outline can serve to jog your memory and keep you on task.

People don't come to hear you speak, only to have you standing with your back to them reading from the projector screen. They want to be entertained. Entertain them.

"Are you not entertained!?" – Russell Crowe – Gladiator

8. Use Your Voice and Hands Effectively. Omit Nervous Gestures

Nonverbal communication carries most of the message. Good delivery does not call attention to itself, but instead conveys the speaker's ideas clearly and without distraction. Good delivery keeps the audience engaged and focused on the message.

9. Grab Attention at the Beginning, and Close with a Dynamic End

Do you enjoy hearing a speech start with, "Today I'm going to talk to you about X?" Most people don't. Instead, use a startling statistic, an interesting anecdote, or concise quotation. Conclude your speech with a summary and a strong statement that your audience is sure to remember. Never end a speech or presentation with something along the lines of, "Well, I guess that's it." Or "That's all I have."

> *Tell the audience what you're going to say, say it, and then tell them what you said.*

10. Use Audiovisual Aids Wisely

Too many can break the direct connection to the audience, so use them sparingly. They should enhance or clarify your content, or capture and maintain your audience's attention.

Capturing your Audience's Attention and Keeping it

Being an audience member to a speech that has not drawn your attention, is like listening to Charlie Brown's teacher - Mwha, mwha, mhwamhwamhwa...there are words being put into the ether, but none of them are landing on the audience in a meaningful way. It's just noise that is mildly interrupting your train of thought or what you are reading on your cell phone. There is no way to really command that an audience puts down their cell phone, but the goal should be that everyone finds what is happening right in front of them, what is coming out of your mouth and the performance you are putting on, as more interesting than their own thoughts or cell phones. You want to commandeer their attention. It's sort of like the difference between management and leadership. It is easy to write policies, but it is difficult to get people to want to follow them. It's easy to write a speech, but it's hard to get anyone to want to listen to it and care about it. From the time you are announced, or step on stage to the time you leave, *the Space between*, is filled with leadership and people will remember that time you shared as either positive or negative. Take control of your future and effect your audience positively.

If the audience isn't interested, and if you haven't made yourself or the topic compelling enough, you may as well not even share the information, because no one will remember it and the audience will walk away with a negative response.

It doesn't matter how great your content is if no one is listening or interested. We must make ourselves and the content compelling enough to commandeer the audience's attention.

It isn't enough to have great information. It must be communicated in the right way. It's no different than regular communication in conversations. If what is coming out of your mouth is inconsistent with the presentation style, your message is lost. There are many approaches to capturing your audience. It is important to choose wisely when deciding which approach is best for any given situation.

Tips for Capturing an Audience

1. **Tell a Captivating Story to Open** – storytelling is a very comfortable space for humans to occupy. It's the most highly recommended way to capture an audience. We've been listening to, telling and learning from stories for as long as words have been spoken. A story can act as a metaphor for the overall theme of your presentation. It can tie up loose ends, it can summarize your point and all the while,

entertain your audience. Remember, a good story has details, action and a clear concise point.

2. **Ask a Rhetorical, Thought Provoking Question** – this tactic can get your audience to think about what you are going to tell them. It sort of greases the wheels so the information you are about to share is more easily digestible. For example if you are speaking on the effect climate change has on humans, you could ask,

> *How do we, as humans, stop ourselves from drowning*
> *in our own naivety and arrogance?*

Of course, we have to provide them with the answer or solution to your question.

3. **State a Shocking Statistic or Headline** – The headline or statistic should shed light on the subject you are going to discuss. It should leave people wanting to hear your explanation or summary. It is also great to follow-up with an audience poll like, "Raise your hand if you agree with this statement." This lets you take the pulse of the audience and see how many people need to be convinced. As it relates to climate change,

17 of the 18 warmest years on record have occurred since 2000.

4. **Use a Powerful Quote** – choose either a well-known person that will add credibility to what you are saying, or an unknown person's quote that exactly exemplifies your point and direction you are going with the information you are sharing. If you are talking about leadership in relation to climate change, a quote from a prominent figure or business leader can add power to the angle you are addressing.

For example - **Proverbs 29:18 – God – known
as the creator of all things**
"Where there is no vision, the people perish."
or
General Ban Ki-moon United Nations Secretary

"Climate change is intrinsically linked to public health, food and water security, migration, peace, and security. It is a moral issue. It is an issue of social justice, human rights and fundamental ethics. We have a profound responsibility to the fragile web of life on this Earth, and to this generation and those that will follow."

5. **Show a Photo** – for example, I spoke about Theory X at a conference, (The Catwalk Conference) which if you remember from Chapters 1 and 4, is the idea that employee's don't want to work, are lazy and need controls and constant oversite to be productive. Does the following photo illustrate all of that and then some? Does it illustrate the point without even having to speak about it? Does it disarm the audience and lighten up the discussion? Might you even get a laugh?

6. **Use a Prop or Creative Visual Aid** - a creative prop or visual aide can capture the audience's attention and even direct that attention toward what you want them to focus on. For example, if you were to speak on climate change – you could use a dramatic representation of the differences in the ice sheets in Antarctica. Maybe you have a quarter and a dime at everyone's seat. You could start by saying, "How many of you knew you were going to be paid to be here today." Attention grabber. Then you ask them to pick up the dime and lay it directly over the quarter. "The quarter is the size of the ice shelf in 1950 and the dime is the size of the ice shelf in 2018. Money is a resource and so is water – and much of our water is being lost due to ice melt and evaporation. If you were losing money at this rate, would you do something about it?"

7. **Play a Short Video** – videos are great if they are used to propel, substantiate or validate the point you are making. They cannot

be the main actor, but should be a terrific supporting actor in your performance. The videos you choose should have the same characteristics within them that you are trying to convey in your own presentation.

In Conclusion

Speaking in Public is scary and may always cause weak knees and palpitations in your chest. Understand that this is normal, but also understand that nervousness can be controlled by a few things: Practice your material. Know it, and be able to talk about it without notes. This leads to confidence and if you can be confident in your ability, you're able to be more authentic – your true self. Understand that content is only one aspect of the presentation, and is useless if the audience isn't interested. Grab their attention and hold it. You want them to remember you and the time you spent with them favorably and have a positive emotional reaction when they remember that mutual time. Ask them to raise their hands for informal polls. Engage them. Get them to listen and want to differentiate themselves from other audience members.

CHAPTER 10

✦ ✦ ✦ **CHAPTER 10** ✦ ✦ ✦

EMPLOYMENT LAW AND INTERVIEWING EFFECTIVELY

(Hire Hard So We Can Manage Easy)

A Brief Introduction

ONE COULD ARGUE THAT THIS section could be covered first in any leadership discussion, because having the right people from the onset is much easier than training, or developing the wrong person to be right, after the fact. The fundamental aspect to developing and creating a lasting team of people who will work together for the right reasons and strive for positive results is **Staffing,** which is the mutual process by which the individual and the organization become matched to form the employment relationship. (Heneman, Heneman, Judge, 4)

However, most leaders do not have the luxury of hiring their staff from the inception of their department. Most leaders are not in a start-up mode; they are scrambling and trying to fill vacancies for staffing fluidity. **Staffing fluidity** is to minimize turnover, and maximize retention. This in turn cuts down on orientation costs, downtime from staff, inconsistency in service, and provides a more secure and functional work unit. It is no different than a sports team trying to put a new player into the lineup each week. The new player is more likely to run the wrong play simply due to inexperience with the team and unfamiliarity with the playbook. The great teams that find tremendous success have stable members that know each other's work patterns, and habits. They know what to expect and uncertainty and ambiguity are diminished.

Just like in the process of Change Management, we want to invest our effort at the front- end of the employment relationship so that the change or new employee takes hold, prospers and grows. We want to **Hire Hard So We Can Manage Easy** which simply put is to invest our effort and energy during the interview process so that we make good, long lasting hiring decisions to avoid doing it again three months later, or have to manage and discipline a person with a bad attitude, poor work performance or skills. The worst place for a department or team to be in is that members are coming and going all the time. This creates uncertainty and unfamiliarity and inhibits growth by the team members who are left behind training the new people with limited resources due to turnover.

Invest time, energy and thoughtfulness at the front-end of the hiring process for long-term dividends in the form of fluidity, teamwork and consistency.

Think of the hiring process as an opportunity to invest in your department's future, the continuity of the team, and the organization. It is not unlike a retirement investment. You want to make the right decision at the front-end and invest in a stock or employee that has a proven track record that fits your needs and will provide a long-term dividend in the form of continued growth, employment and a return on your investment at the back-end.

To mirror the hiring process as an investment, we want to find the right person that will fit your department's needs, while at the same time the department and team will fit the candidate's needs and provide long-term stability to each. The relationship has to be mutually beneficial or it will not work.

A side effect of proper hiring and finding the correct fit is that the leader has more time to focus on the higher order needs of the department. If we compare staffing to **Maslow's Needs Hierarchy of**

Motivation, staffing is like providing the basic needs for employees such as food, water, shelter and safety. Employees who are in a department that is constantly turning over and hiring new employees can't even reach the 3rd level or (social level) in the needs hierarchy due to constantly seeing new people and never really ever being able to get acquainted with them. It's very difficult to fulfill social, self-esteem and self-actualization needs when the daily work-life is tumultuous, unsteady and uncertain.

The ultimate goal of staffing is to provide stability so that leaders and employees can focus on higher order need fulfillment, such as quality improvement, client satisfaction and ultimately their own self-esteem and self-actualization which of course lends itself to others around them finding theirs. .

Federal Anti-Discrimination Laws

First and foremost in the hiring process, we want to do it legally and ensure everyone who applies is considered for employment without bias. Over the years, and because of employer abuse of employees, the federal government has put into place hundreds and maybe thousands of pieces of legislation for the protection of employees.

The main trend with all of these laws is to prevent discrimination due to prejudice. To clarify the difference between prejudice and discrimination, **Prejudice** is a preconceived judgment or opinion, an adverse opinion or leaning formed without just grounds or before sufficient knowledge. (Websters) This is first and foremost what employment law is trying to avoid in the interview and hiring process. Prejudice can lead to discrimination which is ultimately what causes employment laws to be broken. To **Discriminate** is to make a difference in the treatment or favor on a basis other than individual merit, i.e, in favor of friends, or against a certain nationality. (Websters)

Prejudice is an irrational idea that passes judgment unsubstantiated, and discrimination is acting on that prejudice.

Employment laws are intended to prevent discrimination. However, only the mind of each individual decision maker can decide that they will not assign characteristics to a group without fully understanding the individual. Discrimination doesn't occur without prejudice and only the individual can decide whether they will or will not view a certain group, person or process without prejudice. Below are various employment laws that attempt to prevent discrimination and regardless of your personal experiences, you must obey them.

A. **Equal Employment Opportunity (EEO)** - refers to the treatment of individuals in all aspects of employment; hiring, promotion, training, termination, etc, in a fair and nonbiased manner. Every employer is bound by the EEO. This is a general statement that reflects the intent to remain unbiased in the employment relationship.

Hire for knowledge, skills and abilities, not other non-job related factors.

B. **Fair Labor Standards Act, 1938** - provides for a minimum wage and a maximum work week in which time over this maximum of 40 hours has to be paid at time and half. This act prohibits children from working before the age of 14 unless it is farm work. Children ages 14-15 cannot work in a hazardous occupation and cannot work more than 3 hours during a school day and 8 hours on a non-school day.

C. **The Equal Pay Act of 1963** – Requires all employees covered by the Fair Labor Standards Act and others to provide equal pay for equal work, regardless of sex.

Equal pay for equal work – performance is the differentiator, not gender.

D. **Title VII of the Civil Rights Act of 1964 and 1991** – Prohibits the discrimination of employment on the basis of race, color, religion, sex and national origin. Title VII of the Civil Rights Act of 1964 created the Equal Employment Opportunity Commission (EEOC) to enforce this act. The EEOC is the governing body that investigates and passes judgment on claims of discrimination. The Civil Rights

Act of 1991 provides compensatory, punitive damages and jury trials in cases involving intentional discrimination and requires employers to demonstrate that job practices are job-related and consistent with business necessities. **Business Necessity** is a work related practice that is necessary to the safe and efficient operation of an organization. A **Bona Fide Occupational Qualification (BFOQ)** is the exception and it is a characteristic providing a legitimate reason why an employer can exclude persons from otherwise illegal basis of consideration. (Mathis, Jackson, 77) For example, a male actor cannot file a claim of discrimination, if the role they auditioned for was for a female. Every claim is investigated.

Discrimination and Ethics

As you've likely picked up I left healthcare with a bad taste in my mouth. I not only left with a bad taste, but I left with two law suits squarely in the middle of my desk. One was for 1 million dollars and the other was for 2 million dollars. It was a major factor in why I left this company. They were the second largest healthcare corporation in the country with over 100,000 employees.

A report had come in that a practice manager had overheard a cardiologist say awful things about his staff. He said, to another staff member, "I can't stand these fat, lazy, f*cking, n*gger, b*tches." She called me. I followed up with her and other office staff independently and privately. I verified that two others also heard the comments. One of the woman was African American, one was half Puerto Rican and half African American, and the other was half Caucasian and half African American. I took what I had found to my CEO with a recommendation to either suspend or terminate the Cardiologist pending his response.

She said, "He's the six million dollar man." And he was. He was paid six million dollars a year, which meant the income he provided to the hospital would have likely been somewhere between a third to a half greater than his salary. She said, "Let me think about this." A day later, I followed up with her. I asked, "Where's your head on Dr. Blank? She said, "He said he didn't say it." I said, "Of course he said that. Every murderer that's ever sat on the stand and had three witnesses point at him as the man who pulled the trigger has said they were innocent. Courts of law don't care that the murder says he's innocent."

Due to the seriousness of this, I contacted the corporate attorney. She demanded we speak to the physician. She recommended a suspension at minimum. The CEO argued with her and somehow convinced her that a written warning would be effective. The CEO and I went to see the physician. I went through the evidence and he said, "I didn't say it, why would I say that, I'm a brown man. I'm from Pakistan. I wouldn't do that." I asked, "Do you think these woman are starting a conspiracy against you?" He said, "Maybe." The CEO minimized the event and clearly took his side over the three woman who had been treated so poorly. This was the final straw to a long list of issues that I had documented regarding his behavior and treatment.

A couple months later, after he acted out again, the two lawsuits came in. They came in the day before I walked away. I opened them and left them sitting directly in the middle of my desk. The math was easy to do as to why he remained, but the part that I couldn't reconcile was the morality, ethics and inhumanity of the situation. I don't know what happened, but likely it was a settlement for a fraction of the suit.

E. **The Equal Employment Opportunity Act of 1972** –Amended Title VII of the Civil Rights Act of 1964 and strengthened the EEOC's enforcement powers and extends coverage of Title VII to government employees, employees in higher education, and other employers and employees.

F. **Pregnancy Discrimination Act of 1978** – Broadens the definition of sex discrimination to include pregnancy, childbirth, or related medical conditions. It prohibits employers from discriminating against pregnant women in employment benefits, or hiring decisions if they are capable of performing their job duties.

> *Pregnancy is not a limitation on employment and is not a factor in employment decisions.*

G. **Age Discrimination in Employment Act of 1967 (ADEA)**- was initiated to protect workers over 40 years of age against discrimination based on age in the areas of hiring, retention, promotion, compensation, and other areas of employment for companies with over 20 employees. It makes it illegal to require retirement to save on pension funding, to replace them with younger workers to save on wages, or pass over them for promotions. This act applies to any employer subject to Title VII. It also bans mandatory retirement before the age of 70.

Age is not a limitation, or predictor of a candidate's performance.

H. **Americans with Disabilities Act of 1990 (ADA)** - This act extends coverage of the civil rights act of 1964. Employers cannot discriminate against any applicant with a disability that substantially limits this person's mental or physical ability. Of course this person has to be able to perform the essential functions of the job. Employers must provide **reasonable accommodation** (which is an attempt to adjust the working conditions or schedule for employees with disabilities) for any person who states they have a disability and can prove this disability and as long as the accommodation doesn't provide an **undue hardship** on the company. I.e. installing an elevator for a person without legs is not a reasonable accommodation, but moving an office to the first floor is. A disabled person is "any person who:

1. Has a physical or mental impairment which substantially limits one or more of such person's **major life activities** – walking, talking, seeing, hearing, etc 2. Has a record of such impairment, or 3. Is regarded as having such an impairment.

Non-Discriminatory and Discriminatory Interview Questions

Interview Questions - Do's and Don'ts

Category	Non-Discriminatory Questions	Discriminatory Questions	Reasoning
National Origin	What is your name? Do you speak any foreign languages that may help?	Is that name Irish?	It doesn't matter where they are from. Violates Title VII.
Age	Are you over 18?	How old are you?	Age is only a consideration if the candidate is under 18.
		What is your date of birth?	Violates ADEA. FLSA has different requirements for children under 18.
Gender	Don't say anything unless it is a BFOQ.	Do you go by Mr. of Ms.?	Gender doesn't matter.
			Could violate Equal Pay Act, EEO act, Pregnancy Discrimination Act.
Race	Don't say anything.	What is your race?	Race doesn't matter. Violates Title VII, EEO Act.
Disabilities	Are you disabled in any way that may affect job performance?	Do you have any physical defects?	Reasonable accommodations are to be made if possible. Violates ADA.
Height and Weight	Inappropriate unless it is a BFOQ.	How tall are you? How much do you weigh?	Doesn't matter. You can not base a hiring decision on height and weight.
Residence	What is your address? How long have you lived there?	Who do you live with? What are the names of the people you live with?	Hiring decisions cannot be based on marital status or if the candidate has children.
Religion	An employee needs to know what the required work schedule is.	Are you religious? What is your faith?	Some religions do not allow work on certain days. Religion is not a factor, but availability is.
Military Record	Have you had military experience or training related to position?	Were you honorably discharged?	Cannot ask what type of discharge was received. May indicate a disability.
Education and Experience	Where did you attend school?	Is that school affiliated with any religion?	Religion is not related
	What experience do you have?	When did you graduate?	May indicate age and violates ADEA.
	Why did you leave prior employment? What was your salary?	What are your hobbies?	Hobbies are irrelevant.
Criminal Record	Have you been convicted of a crime?	Have you been arrested?	There is a big difference between a conviction and an arrest.
Citizenship	Are you legally able to work in the United States?	Are you a U.S. citizen?	Being a U.S. citizen is not relevant because visas can be issued that allow non-citizens to work in the U.S.
Marital/Family Status	Who can we contact in case of an emergency	Are you married, divorced, single? Do you prefer Miss, Ms. or Mrs.?	Employment decisions can not be based on these issues.
		Do you have any children?	Irrelevant to be successful in job.

Interviewing Hard so you can Manage Easy

To accomplish our ultimate goal with staffing, which is to hire qualified people who are a good fit in the department and organization, we want to ensure we uncover all the stumbling blocks to employment before we make the job offer. It is so much easier to make a good investment at the front-end and watch it grow and pay back dividends in fluidity, teamwork and consistency. The strategies below will help guide us through this process so that we can make good, long lasting and mutually beneficial employment decisions.

10 Interviewing Strategies

The proper way to go into an interview is to make no assumptions and let the facts persuade you. The intangibles such as non-verbal cues, enthusiasm or lack of enthusiasm should be deciding factors between candidates that share an equivalent skill set. Remember, after minimum qualifications, fit is the key.

The following list presents ten guidelines for employment interviews that are commonly accepted and supported by research findings. Their apparent simplicity should not lead one to underestimate their importance.

1. **Establish an interview plan** – Examine the purposes of the interview and determine the areas and specific questions to be covered. Review job requirements, application-form data, and other available information before seeing the applicant. Look for questionable information in the application and resume and seek to gain understanding and clarification.

2. **Establish and maintain rapport** – This is accomplished by greeting the applicant pleasantly, by explaining the purpose of the interview, by displaying sincere interest in the applicant, and by listening carefully.

The more comfortable a candidate is during an interview,
the more likely they will show you their true selves.

3. **Be an active listener** – Strive to understand, comprehend, and gain insight into what maybe suggested or implied. A good listener's mind is alert, and their face and posture reflect this fact. Refer to Chapter 3 on *Effective Communication*.

The interview isn't about you. It's about the candidate, so stop talking and listen to them. If you are talking the whole time, of course you are going to like the candidate. Everyone likes to be listened to.

4. **Pay attention to nonverbal cues** – An applicant's facial expressions, gestures, body position, and movements often provide clues to that person's attitudes and feelings. Interviewers should be aware of what they are communicating nonverbally as well. We need to trust what those non-verbal cues tell us. I.e. body language, space language, paralanguage, and of course time language. If they are late, or do not have a sense of urgency – this can be a predictor of a future problem.

Non-verbal cues are the most ancient form of human communication, trust your gut.

5. **Provide information as freely and honestly as possible** – Answer fully and frankly the applicant's questions. Give the candidate a **Realistic Job Preview**, which details both the negatives and positives of the position. The point in giving the candidate the pros and cons of the job are so they can make an informed decision and hopefully a decision that will last. It doesn't make sense to the leader, candidate or potential co-workers to mislead or withhold information from a candidate. If they find out the job isn't what you told them, they will feel resentment, betrayal, and certainly a loss of confidence and trust in you as their leader.

On the other hand, if you as their leader, "shoot straight," and tell them the full scope of the position, they will gain trust and confidence in your word and there will be no discrepancies in expectations. Besides, you don't want to trick someone into accepting a job, make them miserable and then find yourself doing the same "song and dance" to replace this person in a month or more.

Tell the candidate the good, the bad and the ugly.

Realistic Job Preview

One company I work with requires people to be in harsh conditions. Our recruiter uses the following informational sheet at the time of the interview. We have the candidate acknowledge they are aware and ok with the environment and expectations. We would assume not hire someone rather than go through the expense, time and effort to hire someone just so they can feel duped when they arrive on the job site. These are harsh conditions, and could be a deal breaker for some people. Isn't it better to know this before we spend time, money and effort bringing them on board just to have them quit.

_____ -The work environment could be loud, dusty, wet, cold, hot, and dirty and often requires elevation to heights, underground work, and confined spaces.

_____ -Climbing, kneeling, reaching, stretching, twisting, bending and walking are required.

_____ -Lifting, pushing, pulling up to 75 lbs may be required on a regular basis.

_____ -Overtime may be required.

_____ -Out of town work may be required including overnight and extended stays.

_____ -Weekend work may be required.

_____ -Nightshift work may be required

Please print and sign acknowledging that you understand the expectations of this position and that you are able to meet these requirements.

_____   _____
Employee (Print)   Employee (Signature)

Date:_____

_____   _____

Manager conducting interview
(Print)

Manager conducting interview
(Signature)

Date:_____

6. **Use Questions** – To elicit a truthful answer, questions should be phrased as objectively as possible, giving no indication of what response is desired. You don't want to "lead the witness," or suggest by the way you ask the question what the correct or desired response is. You want honest responses that will weed out candidates that may not be a good fit.

Don't lead the candidate to the answer you want to hear.

7. **Separate facts from inferences** – During the interview, record factual information. Later, record your inferences or interpretations of the facts. Compare your inferences with those of other interviewers. Do not make assumptions. If you need clarification or there is inconsistency, just ask the person more questions to gain clarity. This is often where the real information is shared – through a follow-up question.

We all know about assumptions.

8. **Recognize biases and stereotypes** – One typical bias is for interviewers to consider strangers who have interests, experiences, and backgrounds similar to their own to be more acceptable. Stereotyping involves forming generalized opinions of how people of a given gender, race, or ethnic background appear, think, feel and act. The influence of sex-role stereotyping is central to sex discrimination in employment. Avoid the influence of "beautyism." Discrimination against unattractive people is a persistent and pervasive form of employment discrimination. Also avoid the "halo effect" or judging an individual favorably or unfavorably overall on the basis of only one strong point (or weak point – horn effect) on which you place high/low value.

Diversity is the spark of innovation.

9. **Control the course of the interview** – Establish an interview plan and stick to it. Provide the applicant with ample opportunity to talk, but maintain control of the situation in order to reach the interview objectives. Sometimes it is advisable to let the candidate get off track so they can feel comfortable, and sometimes what they share is enlightening, but always come back to asking for an answer to the original question.

10. **Standardize the questions asked** – To increase reliability and avoid discrimination, ask the same questions of all applicants for a particular job. Keep careful notes; record facts, impressions, and any relevant information, including what was told to the applicant.

Potential Problems in the Interview

Our goal during an interview is to mine accurate and useful information without bias so we can make the best decisions for our departments and companies. We want to ensure that what we believe about a person after an interview is as close to the truth as possible. In essence, we are trying to use the interview to predict the future performance of a candidate. This is difficult, but consistency in comparing apples to apples is critical. Evidence indicates that interviewers make perceptual judgments that are often inaccurate. (Agreement among interviewer's ratings are poor; that is, they have different conclusions about the applicant.)

"Interviewers generally draw early impressions that become very quickly entrenched. If negative information is exposed early in the interview, it tends to be more heavily weighted than if that same information comes out later. Studies indicate that most interviewers' decisions change very little after the first four to five minutes of the interview. As a result, information elicited early in the interview carries greater weight than does information elicited later, and a "good applicant," is probably

characterized more by the absence of unfavorable characteristics than by the presence of favorable characteristics." (Robbins, 128.)

Below are some interviewing pitfalls to be aware of and try to avoid. The goal is to remain unbiased and stay focused throughout the entire interview. Do not pass judgment until the candidate leaves the office. It is also beneficial to ask other's opinions, such as the receptionist, or others who may have had contact with the candidate.

During an interview the candidate should talk and the interviewer should listen.

Snap Judgments – Some interviewers decide whether an applicant is suitable within the first four to five minutes of the interview and spend the rest of the time looking for evidence to support their judgment. This can also work in the other direction – if an employer really needs someone they may see only what they want to see in an attempt to fill a position with a poorly qualified applicant who isn't a good fit, just because they need a quick fix. The issue is that a quick fix doesn't take into account the negative impact of a bad a hire; more attention to management, performance correction, dragging down the work of good employees around the bad hire and demotivating them with their poor performance. It simply put, lowers the bar or excellence.

Negative emphasis – When evaluating suitability, unfavorable information about an applicant is often emphasized more than favorable information. This could be related to a leader's tendency toward the Theory X or Theory Y style of management.

Self-Serving Bias – The tendency for individuals to attribute their own successes to internal factors while placing blame for failures on external factors. Be careful not to disparage other departments, or people. On the flipside, you want to look for the candidate's ability to take responsibility for their own actions. This is how people learn and grow. If they are always blaming others, the likelihood that they will ever see themselves in need of growth or change is very small.

Halo Effect – occurs when an interviewer allows a positive characteristic, such as agreeableness, to overshadow other evidence. For example, if a person turns out incredible amounts of quality work, but cannot get along with people, their appraisal scores will still reflect positively in all aspects of their work as if they do not have interpersonal issues.

Devil's Horn - describes the reverse of the halo effect; this occurs when a negative characteristic, such as inappropriate dress, or poor style, overshadows other traits. For example, if an employee is well liked by his/her peers, complies with work rules, yet doesn't produce a quality product, yet their appraisal scores are all negative because of their production.

Projection – It's easy to judge others if we assume they're similar to us. For instance, if you want challenge and responsibility in your job, you assume that others want the same. Or, if you're honest and trustworthy, you assume that other people are equally honest and trustworthy. This tendency to attribute one's own characteristics to other people can distort perceptions.

Biases and stereotyping – Similarity bias occurs when interviewers favor or select people that they believe to be like themselves based on a variety of personal factors. Interviewers also should avoid any personal tendencies to stereotype individuals because of demographic characteristics or differences. For instance, age disparities may be a concern as young executives are interviewing more senior personnel. Additionally, applicants' ethnic names and accents can negatively impact personal evaluations, and older workers are sometimes less likely to get interviewed and hired than are younger applicants. This is not only illegal, but you may be missing out on a great employee.

Go into the interview with no preconceived notions. Remember, different than you isn't an indicator or predictor of good or bad performance, it's simply an indication that they may see things differently than you. Embrace diversity and use it for creativity and innovation, not homogenization which tends to lead to groupthink which tends to lead to poor decisions.

Types of Questions to Avoid in the Interview Process

These types of questions don't really turn over any rocks, and don't dig into the real person. At the end of the interview you want to feel like you walked into a field full of stones and turned them all over. You want to know as much as possible about the person's potential, past, and present performance. The past is a great predictor of the future. The types of questions below will hinder our ability to gain insight into the person's potential behavior.

Yes/No Questions – Unless verifying specific information, the interviewer should avoid questions that can be answered with "yes" or "no."

Obvious questions – An obvious question is one for which the interviewer already has the answer and the applicant knows it. This makes the interviewer look unprepared and uneducated.

Questions that rarely produce a true answer – avoid questions that prompt a less-than-honest response. An example is, "how did you get along with co-workers?" The likely answer is, "just fine," but this also presents an opportunity to dig a little deeper.

Leading questions – a leading question is one to which the answer is obvious from the way the question is asked. An example is, "Isn't this area of the country great?" Clearly the interviewer believes it is, so it would be in the candidate's best interest to answer in the affirmative. You could ask the same question without leading the candidate like this, "What do you think about this area of the country?"

Illegal questions – as discussed in the do's and don'ts of interview questions above. Stick to job related questions.

Questions that are not job related – All questions should be directly job related to ensure legality, and to steer clear of bias.

Different Types of Interviews

Structured Interview – an interview that uses a set of standardized questions asked to all applicants. This is important for consistency sake so that each applicant has the opportunity to answer the same questions and hiring managers can compare the answers of the various candidates equally. If consistency is not present, the possibility of a discrimination claim becomes more likely.

Behavioral Interview – applicants are asked to describe how they have performed a certain task or handled a problem in the past, which may predict future actions and show how applicants are best suited for the current job. An example may be, "Tell me about a time when you were able to inspire others to act. How did you do this? What was the outcome?"

Situational Interview – contains questions about how applicants might handle specific job situations. The interviewer typically codes the suitability of the answer, assigns point values, and adds up the total number of points each candidate received.

Non-directive Interview – Uses questions developed from the answers to previous questions. The interviewer asks general questions designed to prompt applicants to describe themselves. The interviewer then uses applicants' responses to shape the next question. The problem with this can be that it is difficult to stay job related, and obtaining comparable data on various applicants. (Mathis, Jackson, 231-232)

In an interview, one would never dismiss the intuition of the interviewer as it relates to their department's needs, but coupling intuition with quantifiable data is critical. If your intuition says, "no," trust it, but it must be verified against the scores from the interview.

Minimum qualifications are paramount, but a good fit is what makes a team. If you have five, seven foot tall centers on a basketball team, your team will likely suffer from lack of quickness, dribbling, and shooting. However, five players who have complementary skills and abilities, like the ability to bring the ball up the court, the ability to shoot well from distance and quickness to guard the smaller, quicker players on other teams, then you have a competitive team.

The leader needs to analyze their team and determine the areas of weakness, whether it's a better ball handler, rebounder, passer, scorer, shooter and then work to fill those gaps. Focus on bringing in strengths through the hiring process to round out the entire team's strengths.

You are the team leader, and you need to understand where gaps exist so you can work to close them through the staffing process.

CHAPTER 11

✦ ✦ ✦ CHAPTER 11 ✦ ✦ ✦

DOCUMENTATION, INVESTIGATIONS, CORRECTIVE ACTION AND APPRAISALS

A Brief Overview

ON THE SURFACE, THE FOUR dimensions of Leadership and Management this chapter will discuss may seem unrelated. However, the similarity that each of these have with the other is that we must not show **bias,** which is the human tendency to make systematic decisions in certain circumstances based on cognitive factors or an inclination to present or hold a partial perspective at the expense of (possibly equally valid) alternatives.

Anything biased is generally one-sided, and therefore lacks a neutral point of view. Bias can come in many forms and is often considered to be synonymous with prejudice (see Chapter 10 for clarification on prejudice) rather than evidence. Secondly, we need to remain **objective,** which is the ability to judge fairly. Objectivity is the opposite of **subjectivity,** which is a person's personal perspective, feelings, beliefs, desires or discovery, as opposed to those made from an independent, objective point-of-view.

These two factors, objectivity and a nonbiased point-of-view are important to the success or failure of Documentation, Investigations, Corrective Action and Appraisals. If an employee senses that their supervisor may play favorites, or if their supervisor has a world view similar to one employee and not another, the likelihood of bias and subjectivity creeping in is heightened. If an employee feels that they are not being, "given a fair shake," they will act out accordingly, (refer to expectancy theory and equity theory from Chapter 4 on Motivation for a refresher on these two concepts.)

An employee must know that any investigation which leads to corrective action and ultimately an employee's appraisal will be conducted impartially, and that corrective and appraisals are administered the same as any other similarly situated employee.

An employee's perception of bias or subjectivity is as real to them as actual bias.

The outcome of just one employee feeling like they were treated unfairly is sometimes catastrophic to a department or unit. The employee will often spend a majority of their day explaining to everyone else just how wicked their leader is. When this happens, if an employee is not objective and nonbiased themselves it is very easy for a swath of negativity to be cut through the middle of a department or team. Sides are taken and factions, like a fissure in stone, occur.

However, a leader's main objective is to help people grow so they can develop. The investigation, discipline and appraisal process should not be one of conflict or confrontation; it should be viewed as an opportunity to assist an employee that we must assume wants to do what is right.

A leader should help people grow. Take a caring, compassionate, and concerned attitude when performing an investigation, corrective action or appraisal.

At the end of an investigation, corrective action or appraisal session the employee should walk away feeling energized, motivated and compelled to do better. Too often leaders look at corrective action and appraisals as something they do not like to perform. The following pages will help leaders gain understanding so that they may view these "unfortunate" aspects of their jobs as an "opportunity" to help employees grow.

Documentation

The need for documentation is often spawned by a report or complaint from an employee, or client. This then sparks a series of events that must be followed to get to the other side of the investigation smoothly, objectively and accurately. Below are a few housekeeping issues that will allow leaders to navigate the documentation process cleanly.

Desk-File – each leader should have a desk file for each employee they work with. This will allow the leader to make notes, and keep a running total of documented issues that the employee encounters. It is very important that not only negative notes and comments are stored in the desk-file, but positive comments as well. This will help the leader be objective and see an accurate picture of the whole employee, not just the issue at hand. This is often most effective if done via spreadsheet.

Proper Record Keeping in Desk-File – collecting information is critical to the idea of objectivity, however the information you collect must be useful. Useful information about a situation or event contains:

1. Date, time and location of event – as specifically as possible.
2. What was the behavior – describe the situation or problem.
3. Why this behavior was a problem or why was it exceptional.
4. Be diligent with this – nothing is too large or too small to document.
5. Make sure your notes are clear and concise so when you review them later, they make sense.

Also critical to the on-going documentation of employee behavior is that you record observations, comments and terrific performances while using the above criteria. This will help when it comes to appraisals and corrective action if necessary and you will have a year's worth of notes to use for the appraisal. This process will also help defend the organization in the event of litigation. Generally though, objective, unbiased, clear and concise documentation practices are the key to avoiding a lawsuit all together.

Investigations

Investigations heighten the sensitivity of employees even when they are not involved, and only act as witnesses. The way a leader handles an investigation can determine the way employees feel toward the leader. Remember everything we do in the Infinite Space between Management and Skill Set is observed, noted and remembered. To be unbiased and honest during investigations, appraisals, and corrective action will gain the leader respect. If a leader appears to be "out to get someone," employees often ban together to protect the employee under investigation.

Investigations will more often than not take wild twists and turns. During an investigation the pendulum will swing back and forth, and the idea of guilt or innocence will become muddy. This is when we need to dig deeper to understand what exactly happened and why. It isn't uncommon for an employee to report an incident that they have some responsibility for, first, like a child telling on their sibling so that they are heard first and then the other person is put on the defensive. There are always two sides.

A coin has two sides, but the value is in the middle.

Some practical applications to avoid bias or subjectivity are to follow these simple guidelines.

Investigation Guidelines – these can be used to ensure the process of investigating a complaint will be fair, objective and accurate.

1. **Determine the Scope** - Identify witnesses, and collect relevant data.
2. **Have a Witness Present** – When interviewing employees under investigation, or who are witnesses to an event, always have a non-partial witness present for your protection, and the employees. This also can help validate the notes and conversations you have with the employee in the future if necessary.

3. **Discretion** – Ask employees to come to your office personally, not over the intercom system or in front of other employees. Ask employees being investigated or witnesses to an event to keep the conversation confidential. Explain to them the importance of this and that they are a very important piece to moving forward.

4. **Leading Questions** – Do not ask leading questions that indicate to the employee or witness the answer you are looking for. Ask open-ended questions like, "Have you witnessed any behavior recently that would cause you to identify a problem or that has caused you concern?" If the employee or witness doesn't respond, only then do you get into the specifics of the incident that is under investigation, but deal out the facts slowly and incrementally as to not steer the witness.

5. **Collect Facts** – We are not interested in opinions, suppositions, or inferences. We want to know what happened and why, not what may have happened or what an employee thought happened.

6. **Document Findings** – Refer to the above section on documentation. Most importantly record the date, time and location of the event.

7. **Review Facts** – Be certain that what has been reported is accurate. Do not let other issues of performance interfere with the situation at hand.

An Excellent way ensure you are obtaining unbiased information is to ask people to write a statement detailing what they remember about the incident or situation under investigation. The below form is an excellent tool to concisely obtain information. If you try to take notes, the information given is often delivered out of order, scattered or in fragments. This form will cause the person providing information to think through what they want to say in a logical sequential order.

* Please document as thoroughly as possible. To ensure the important details are included, please include dates, times, names, places and specific details related to the incident. Focus on facts and please avoid making any assumptions, inferences or generalizations.
** If you are being asked to document your viewpoint on an issue, please state only what you witnessed.
*** **In accordance with our strict anti-retaliation policy, no retaliation will result from completing this form.**

Manager / Employee Completing   Date Completed

This documentation is most closely related to:

Manager documentation of event   Ethical Issue

Reporting a complaint   Harassment (choose type below)

Witness to an event   Sexual   Hostile

Date of Event   Location of Event   Other people involved/witnesses (First and Last Name)

Time of Incident   Firsthand witness?

          AM   PM   Yes   No

Brief Summary of Issue:

Specific Details of Issue:

Your signature is required. Please know that strict confidentiality will be kept to the extent possible. If more space is needed continue to next page.

Employee Signature: **Date:**

Complaint / Issue / Witness Documentation Form   1

Investigations

There was a report from the Critical Care Unit (CCU) that a family member saw a nurse give her father a pill that was different than the one the day before. I asked the pharmacy to pull records from the automated pharmacy dispenser to see what pills were being dispensed and to whom. I verified the report from the family member with the pharmacist that the pill should have been light blue, but instead the pill the nurse gave her patient was redish/orange.

This prompted an audit of the patient records to see if the medications being administered matched the medications that were being distributed. The records were off by 57 pills per week throughout various units. Unfortunately, the missing pill phenomenon was not as uncommon as everyone would have assumed.

The finger pointed directly at the nurse we suspected. She was about 30 year's old, blonde, attractive and had two kids that were five and seven years old. She came to my office. I had the Director of Security with me. We often played good cop, bad cop in those situations. I was the good cop and he was the bad cop that actually brought into play, the real cops. The nurse's reaction was the same as many of the other nurses that had been caught in the opioid crisis – emotionless. It was the damnedest thing – normally when someone was being questioned or accused of something they react one of two ways - outrage or tears. Very consistently, the people who were actively taking narcotics and/or opioids from patients and ingesting them, showed no emotion until nearly an hour or more into the discussion when the facts being dealt out became overwhelming. The key for us was to get people to admit it. The likelihood of recovery was much better if they did.

During her breakdown, she told us that she substituted OxyContin, Xanax, Percocet, and Valium with Advil. She was adamant that she wasn't selling the pills on the street, but was taking them. She explained that she had knee surgery and the pain didn't subside when her pain prescription ran out. The other commonality was that once the confession started, it didn't stop until all had been purged. She told us that the person who taught her to steal the meds was actually the on-site instructor from the local nursing college that worked with nurses on their preceptor – on-site practical training.

We of course thought this was not true, but to give the investigation its due, looked into it. We pulled the records and sure enough, the link to this nurse was evident. She also went on and told us that her sister had been involved and had diverted pills from patients. She was concerned for her sister's well-being after hearing our spiel on drug addiction, legal ramifications, etc. We traced it back to her as well.

The point is that these things take time, we knew she was guilty, we could have just termed her and moved on, but we wouldn't have gotten to the root of the problem. We wouldn't have been able to increase the likelihood of helping her overcome addiction. It all started with a knee surgery. She wasn't a bad person. She was desperate. Eventually she came out of rehab and worked for the hospital again. The nursing instructor actually came into my office after she finished her treatment program and broke down in tears. She thanked me for treating her with dignity and helping her rather than simply turning her over to the police. Which we did, but we set her up with rehab and were able to tell the police she admitted it, was remorseful and sought treatment. Investigations have many tentacles and spokes. They often take wild turns and sometimes people assumed to be guilty are innocent. Take the time to understand and make the right decision. Your reputation depends on it and the trust and respect of those you serve teeters in the balance. Fill the Infinite Space between the complaint and decision with objectivity, and non-bias.

Corrective Action

Once an employee has been found to have committed some infraction, a leader must handle the current situation the same as other similar situations have been handled. As much as you ask an employee not to talk about their pay, their evaluations, and discipline against them, they do talk about these things. If anything is inconsistent, you have not only jeopardized the trust and respect of employees, but you have also opened the door to discrimination charges.

For example, if an employee was terminated for theft, yet another employee wasn't, and the employee that was terminated falls into a protected class (over 40, female, minority, or disabled) as we discussed in the previous chapter, a court will have a hard time understanding why the person in the protected class was terminated while the white, fit, thirty year old man with no disability was not. The only basis for treating one person differently than another is discrimination, which as we learned is directly related to prejudice and bias.

Corrective action is an opportunity to help an employee see the path they need to take for success. Punishment is not the goal.

It isn't uncommon for a leader to avoid disciplinary action for a variety of reasons. As Mathis and Jackson illustrate below, the reasons can vary greatly, but in no sense are these valid reasons not to take disciplinary action with an employee.

Not taking corrective action with an employee is like condoning the behavior. The culture and commitment of other employees will suffer if poor performers are not addressed.

Common Reasons Why Discipline Might Not Be Used

1. **Organizational Culture of Avoiding Corrective Action** – if the organizational "norm" is to avoid penalizing problem employees, then managers are less likely to use discipline or to terminate problem employees.
2. **Lack of Support** – many managers do not want to use corrective action because they fear that their decisions will not be supported by higher management. The degree of support is also a function of organizational culture.
3. **Guilt** – some managers realize that before they became managers, they committed the same violations as their employees, and therefore do not use corrective action on others for actions they formerly committed.
4. **Fear of Loss of Friendship** – managers may fear losing friendships or damaging personal relationships if they discipline employees.
5. **Avoidance of Time Loss** – corrective action often requires considerable time and effort. Sometimes it is easier for managers to avoid taking the time required for corrective action, especially

if their actions may be overturned on review by higher management. Consult HR when performing corrective actions.

6. **Fear of Lawsuits** – Managers are increasingly concerned about being sued for corrective action with an employee, particularly in regard to the ultimate corrective action step of termination. (Mathis, Jackson, 529)

Perspectives on Discipline and Corrective Action

Discipline/Corrective Action is defined as punishment and control gained by obedience or training. The world of work requires a different approach to this as new generations unfold and spread their wings to start their careers. To **punish** is to impose a penalty against someone. People are often afraid of punishment and their behavior is curtailed to avoid punishment or harsh outcomes. Remember, as Yoda (the Master Jedi) said in the section on Motivation,

Fear creates anger, anger creates hatred and hatred creates suffering.
(Which then leads to increased and often unnecessary turnover.)

We are not interested in blind obedience, or control based on fear or punishment, what we are interested in is commitment to the organizational mission, and people making their own decisions for the right reasons – ideally from a place of intrinsic motivation. Unfortunately, the corrective action process often leaves the employee feeling as if they were just tied to a post and whipped, as if they were acting in a way to actively undermine the organizational goals. This is normally not the case. Employees have bad days, bad ideas, and sometimes execute those bad ideas on bad days. This doesn't mean they are bad and often the employee feels remorse and does not want to do it again.

"Managers often see discipline as part of changing workers' behaviors,
employees often see discipline as unfair because
it can affect their jobs and careers."
(Mathis, Jackson, 528)

Progressive Discipline or Corrective Action

The style of corrective action that is most prevalent in today's business world is somewhat counterintuitive to the creation of high performing employees. We want employees to grow, and get better, not work in fear of failure or punishment. Remember, a climate of innovation and empowerment comes from the freedom to make decisions, fail and adjust. This process could be called a coaching session to gain commitment, not corrective action.

Below is the generally accepted concept of discipline - **progressive discipline** which is the use of corrective measures in increasingly more serious steps. Progressive Discipline incorporates steps that become progressively more stringent and are designed to change the employee's inappropriate behavior. (Mathis, Jackson, 530)

Generally, employees feel at odds with their supervisor during the progressive discipline process. This is unnecessary and can lead to poor attitudes, fear, and morale problems. Progressive discipline is common, but not recommended. We need to understand where we have been so we know where we are going which is why we are going to look at two types of corrective action – progressive discipline is "old school" (there is nothing progressive about it,) and positive discipline which is the preferred way.

Stages of Progressive Discipline or Corrective Action

Generally, it takes a four step approach to correcting a person's behavior. It is a step-by-step process that with each infraction takes the employee one step closer to termination. It is scary to the employee and often seems out of his/her control.

Step 1 – First Offense – Verbal Warning/Caution – it is carried out like this:
The employee comes to the leader's office. They sit down. The leader describes the problem and why it is an infraction and asks the employee to sign the verbal warning.

Step 2 – Second Offense – Written Warning – it is carried out like this: The employee comes to the leader's office. They sit down. The leader describes the problem and that it is the second occurrence. They explain that continued infractions could result in additional disciplinary action up to and including termination of employment. The leader explains why it is an infraction and they ask the employee to sign the written warning.

Step 3 – Third Offense – Suspension – it is carried out like this: The employee comes to the leader's office. They sit down. The leader describes the problem, explains that this is the third occurrence and that continued infractions could result in additional disciplinary action up to and including termination of employment. They explain why it is an infraction and ask the employee to sign the suspension form.

Step 4 – Fourth Offense – Termination – it is carried out like this: The employee comes to the leader's office. They sit down. The leader describes the problem, and that because this is the fourth time, it has led to termination of employment.

Positive or Non-Punitive Discipline

Positive or non-punitive discipline is very different from progressive discipline. Positive discipline requires employees to take responsibility for their actions. It requires employees to evaluate themselves and decide if they can make a commitment to change their behavior or not.

Positive discipline is defined as a system of discipline or corrective action that focuses on the early correction of employee misconduct, with the employee taking total responsibility for correcting the issue. Of course the leader will act as a resource for the employee through the process, but at all times holds the employee fully responsible for their own behavior. The key to a successful positive discipline process is that employees have a clear understanding as to what is expected of them. Just as we will learn in the appraisal process, you can't criticize an employee or discipline them if they are not clear as to what is expected of them. Often leaders assume that employees should understand what expectations are but, as we know, many organizations do things differently and to compound this each leader has different expectations. There are still four steps, but the process is very different.

It is better for an employee to not want to disappoint their leader, rather than fear them. The difference between progressive and positive discipline is fear in the former and disappointment in the latter.

Positive Discipline – Attendance Issue

Step 1 - You would let the employee know that they are approaching their limit for absences. You may say something like, "Hey, I just wanted to let you know that you only have two more unscheduled absences left and we have three more months in the reporting period. Were you aware of this? (Of course, they will say, "Yes.") Good, your co-workers and I need you here at work for the success of our team. You being here is a key component to our success. When someone is absent I'm sure you know how it can affect the entire team's day. Can you commit to staying under the absenteeism limit?" The employee will respond with "Yes," committing to do this. The ball is now in their court.

Step 2 - If absences continue, you may ask them to recommit to addressing this problem. This time you are going to ask for their commitment in writing. You will use the guidelines for documenting employee behavior and ask for their commitment again to correct the problem. Say something to them in a written statement such as "the organization needs your commitment to meet our absenteeism standards. We agreed upon the terms of employment at the time you were hired and we need you to adhere to these commitments." Leave a space for the employee to sign, acknowledging this commitment and make comments. It becomes an informal contract. The employee doesn't want to break their word by failing to meet his or her commitment and if they do, it is their decision and they know the consequences.

Step 3 - And of course occasionally an employee will break their commitment and the attendance problems will resurface. This time the leader will address the issue with a written statement detailing what has happened to this point. The statement will include that the employee has made two prior commitments and failed to honor these commitments of employment and is being asked to take a day off **with or without pay** depending on how the company wants to handle this. They need to decide whether or not this is a behavior that can be immediately corrected or if they need to resign their employment with the organization. The employee will bring the statement back to work the next day and sign it if he or she can make the commitment or resign if they feel they cannot. It is their decision.

Step 4 - If the employee commits to correcting the behavior by signing the statement and the problem persists, then you will be forced to make an employment decision for the employee. Still, there will be no surprises.

Appraisals

There should be no surprises in the appraisal process.

Performance appraisals are intended to measure how well an employee is meeting job requirements and most importantly provide feedback and direction for their continued growth. However, performance appraisals often don't measure or address these items at all. Sometimes they measure how popular an employee is with the leader, or how well the employee has done in the last month, and sometimes they are even measured against other employees rather than against what the job description warrants.

Employees can be blind-sided by poor performance on their appraisal. This should never happen. Employees should know what they are to do and leaders should address problem areas so that the employee doesn't think the behavior is o.k. As we discussed in the Ethics and Recognition chapter, they should also be told about the positive aspects as they occur. There should be no surprises in the evaluation process – good or bad. Remember, employees crave feedback, they want to do well, and it is the leader's job to ensure the employee is aware how their performance is being viewed by their leader and what steps they can take to be great.

Appraisal Guidelines

1. Performance appraisals must be job related.
2. Employees must be given a written copy of their job standards/ job description in advance of appraisals and, ideally, at the time of hire.
3. Leaders who conduct the appraisal must be able to observe the behavior they are rating. This implies having a measurable standard with which to evaluate employee behavior.
4. Leaders must be trained to use the appraisal form correctly. They should be instructed on how to apply appraisal standards when making judgments.

5. Appraisals should be discussed openly with the employees and counseling or corrective guidance offered to help poor performers improve performance.

6. An appeal procedure should be established to enable employees to express disagreement with the appraisal. (Bohlander, Snell)

Potential Pitfalls to Successful and Positive Appraisals

Of course, too often there are surprises and the appraisal process turns into a negative experience for both the leader and employee very quickly. Employees should know what to expect at appraisal time. They should be in contact with their leaders so they are aware of improvement areas prior to being evaluated on those areas. Again, Leaders must fill the Infinite Space between Management and Skill Set with positive input, coaching, teaching and encouragement.

It is unrealistic for an employee to improve performance if they are unaware that performance is suffering. Address issues as they arise and let the employee know what it was about their performance that was substandard and what they can do to improve their performance in a given area.

Reasons Appraisals Sometimes Fail

1. Managers feel that little or no benefit will be derived from the time and energy spent in the process.

2. Managers dislike the face-to-face confrontation of appraisal interviews. This should never be a confrontation if the leader has actively engaged and led the employee between appraisals. (Remember, you are in charge, and it is your responsibility to take an active role in providing guidance, direction and support between appraisals by filling the Infinite Space between appraisals with positive and supportive leadership.

3. Managers are not sufficiently adept in providing appraisal feedback.)

4. The judgmental role of appraisal conflicts with the helping role of developing employees. (Bohlander, Snell) (This is simply not true is judgment is based on observable, measurable goals and if an employee isn't meeting those goals, it is inherent to any leadership role to help the person meet the agreed upon standards.

Performance Appraisals - Rater Errors

Similar to interviewing and the biases that may impede a positive hiring decision, there are many different types of appraisal errors. Each of them can lead to trouble when one or more fall into the employee's appraisal. An employee has a preconceived notion as to what the job duties are but, more accurately, they should be working from a correct and accurate job description because the job description is the basis for performance review. Often these preconceived notions are inaccurate or the proper way to perform a job has not been detailed to the employee, but that is a training issue.

When an employee feels they are performing one way and then their performance appraisal states says otherwise, they feel discontented, disheartened and frustrated. If this occurs, the leader has let the employee down as well as the organization and themselves.

There are many rater errors that can affect performance appraisals and it is important to understand and be able to identify them and, more importantly, avoid them all together. Is it possible to avoid them all together? Yes…but you must have the knowledge, understanding and commitment to do so. These will look familiar to you, but it is important to reiterate the value in avoiding these errors.

Halo Error - occurs when the employee performs outstanding in one area and because of this all other areas are rated outstanding. This could be from focusing too much attention on one aspect of the job and neglecting the rest.

For example, if everyone likes the employee and their interpersonal skills are outstanding but their work is below average and the leader rates them high in all areas because they are so well liked, this error has occurred. It is not fair or appropriate to the employee or co-workers if all aspects of employment are not validly and accurately appraised. It condones poor performance and causes high performers to work toward mediocrity.

Horn Error - occurs the opposite of the halo error in that if one area is poor all areas will be rated poorly.

Error of Central Tendency - is when the appraiser rates all or most of the employees being appraised around the mid-point of the scale. This could occur because the supervisor is afraid to hurt feelings or cause problems. But what this does is de-motivates high performers to work hard and allows low performers to remain low. If mediocrity is your goal, then apply this error, but if you believe that people want to be great and will be great if they are given the correct environment with appropriate leadership, then avoid this and celebrate great and work to improve weak.

The effect of central tendency is to de-motivate people to work hard.

The supervisor or appraiser is not doing the employee or the organization any favors by evaluating everyone as mediocre. They are actually doing a disservice to both. Employees do not know how they are truly doing so there is no motivation to improve. The status quo has been set and you can expect even the good employees to fall to mediocrity.

Leniency or Strictness Error - is when the appraiser scores the employees unusually high or low. Again, the reasoning for this is similar to the error of central tendency. Managers, supervisors and appraisers are either afraid to hurt feelings and score everyone at a higher level than they should, hoping to gain popularity or they feel that no person is perfect and there is always room for improvement. Of course we have to remember that we are working from job descriptions and if an employee far exceeds one aspect of the job description, their evaluation should reflect that excellence just like the converse is true.

Recency Error - is when an employee is rated on recent behavior rather than for the entire appraisal period. For example, if an employee has been producing an incredible amount of work for the last quarter, but has failed to meet standards for the prior three quarters, under this error they may receive an outstanding rating. This is an error.

The evaluation period is for the entire year, not just the last quarter.

Contrast Error - occurs when an employee is rated either higher or lower based on the previous employees rating being either high or low. Under this error, you certainly do not want to be rated after the superstar, especially if you are just meeting standards.

Each employee should be rated based on their job description, not on how they compare to other employees.

Similar–to-me-Error - occurs when the rater evaluates the employee and inflates the rating based on some mutual personal connection. For example, an employee is appraised incredibly high, because the appraiser and the employee share some common interest such as sailing. This error is common when there is favoritism or nepotism.

These errors occur naturally in people because we do judge and come to conclusions without knowing all the facts. The key to avoiding these errors and rating employees on the merit of their performance is to understand the errors, decide you will not let them into the appraisal and work to avoid them.

Appraisal Checklist

Use the checklist below to ensure you are properly executing the performance appraisal and doing what you can to enable the process to be positive.

The appraisal process should be a positive experience for the leader and the employee.

Scheduling

1. Schedule the review and notify the employee ten to fourteen days in advance.
2. Ask the employee to prepare for the session by reviewing his or her performance, job objectives, and development goals in advance.
3. Clearly state that this will be a formal, annual performance appraisal.

Preparing for the Appraisal

1. Review the performance documentation collected throughout the year in your desk file. Concentrate on work patterns that have developed.
2. Be prepared to give specific examples of above, or below-average performance.
3. When performance falls short of expectations, determine what changes need to be made. If performance meets or exceeds expectations, discuss this and plan how to reinforce it.
4. After the appraisal is written, set it aside for a few days and then review it again.

Conducting a Positive Appraisal

1. Select a location that is comfortable and free of distractions. The location should encourage a frank and candid conversation. It is not advisable for the leader to sit behind a desk while the employee sits in front of them. Find a neutral space. We do not want to lord over them from the big chair.
2. Discuss each topic in the appraisal one at a time, consider strengths and short comings.
3. Be specific and descriptive, not general and judgmental. Report occurrences rather than judging them.
4. Discuss your differences and resolve them. Solicit agreement with the evaluation.

5. Jointly discuss and design plans for making improvement for growth and development.

6. Maintain a professional and supportive approach to the appraisal discussion.

Benefits of Proper Appraisal

Allowing rater errors to slip into evaluations could result in a discrimination charge. Training managers to understand rater errors and avoid them will help maintain the unbiased appraisals that lead to success. A biased appraisal will lead to lack of employee motivation and drag everyone to mediocrity. If employees are not evaluated accurately it causes them to feel as if their hard work is for nothing. The reward must match the effort. This inspires effort and improvement. Remember the Chapter on Motivation, expectancy theory states the effort put forth must match the reward offered. If the reward is less than the effort required to obtain the reward, motivation will be low.

Employees and the organization benefit when employees are treated fairly, unbiased and recognized for their effort accurately. When employees are accurately evaluated they are given the opportunity to improve and feel appreciated for their efforts. Ambiguity is diminished and you as their leader have given the employee the tools to succeed and feel good about it once they have improved or met a goal.

In Summary

The overall theme of this book should be evident by this point. Management has evolved into leadership and people have evolved into active and meaningful players in organizations, rather than tools to produce a desired outcome. Work has changed. What people want from work has changed. Ideas about work and works importance to a person's life and identity have changed. Work has become integrated with life through technology. Work has become more sophisticated.

Shovels, chisels, hammers, pulleys, and strong backs have given way to machinery, processes and policies and in some cases, even robots.

People want to be lead, not managed. People want to grow, not be minimized, stunted or marginalized. They want to be valued. They want to feel like they are part of something larger than themselves. They want meaning. They want purpose. It is in "the Infinite Space between Management and Skill Sets" that leaders can have the greatest impact on the well-being, self-actualization and satisfaction of employees. Don't miss an opportunity to lead. These opportunities are present in our interactions, our communications, our ability to listen, and how we recognize, appreciate and approach our employees. Take a compassionate and caring approach and treat people as individuals with big lives that are important to them and therefore important to you because you value people not just as a means to get work done, but a valuable contributor to the overall well-being of the company and society.

It is our responsibility as leaders to provide the best environment possible to enhance the likelihood that an employee will find self-actualization, and then reach for the next goal, not just at work, but in life. We must fill *the Infinite Space between Management and Skill Sets* with leadership that people are willing to follow, respect and emulate when they get the opportunity to lead groups of people. A fully engaged person in their personal life will be more engaged and more likely to push toward success in their professional life. The two should feed one another. We want to create a cycle of positivity that feeds personal and professional lives.

The keys to success are to view each person and situation as an individual. There is no standard approach to inspire people. Because of the infinite number of options available in every situation, we must whittle away the options that are less effective and focus on our own ability to read a situation so we can have the most impact. There are behaviors that people admire. There are tactics that produce outcomes, but there is no blueprint for leadership. Leadership success is attained moment by moment. Leadership failure is also a moment to moment occurrence. Just because at one moment a failure occurs, does not mean the next moment can't be a success. The key is to be open, to be objective, to be emotionally engaged, to be a good listener, to be adaptable, to understand the value of each person, to believe that everyone wants to be great, and to understand that the power to inspire those around us, is within us all and it comes by filling *the Infinite Space between Management and Skill Set* with solid leadership principles that are grounded in the idea that it is our job as the leader to inspire those around us.

BIBLIOGRAPHY

Borchert, M. Donald, Stewart, David II, *Exploring Ethics*, MacMillan Publishing Company, 1986

Daft, L. Richard, Marcic, Dorothy, *Understanding Management*, Harcourt College Publishers, 3rd edition, 2001

Robbins, P. Stevens, *Organizational Behavior*, 10th Edition, Prentice Hall, 2003

Bateman, S. Thomas, Snell A. Scott, *Management, Competing in the New Era*, McGraw-Hill Irwin, 5th edition, 2002

Bohlander, George and Snell, Scott. *Managing Human Resources*, Thomson, Southwestern 13th Edition, 2004

French, Wendell, Human Resources Management, Houghton Mifflin Publishers, 4th Edition, 1998

Lesiker, Raymond.V., Flately, Marie, E., *Basic Business Communication, Skills for Empowering the Internet Generation, 2002*

Guffey, E. Mary, *Essentials of Business Communication*, Thomas, Southwestern, 6th Edition, 2004

Myers, Gail E., Myers, Michelle Tolela, *The Dynamics of Human Communication: A Laboratory Approach*, McGraw-Hill, 6th Edition, 1992

Northouse, G. Peter, *Leadership, Theory and Practice*, Sage Publications, Inc., 2nd Edition, 2001

Kouzes M. James, Posner, Z. Barry, *The Leadership Challenge*, Jossey-Bass, 1997.

Myers, G. David *Psychology*, Worth Publishers, 3rd Edition, 1992

French, L. Wendell, Bell, H. Cecil Jr, *Organizational Development, Behavior Science Interventions for Organization Improvement*, 5th Edition, Prentice Hall, 1995.

Mathis, L. Robert, Jackson, H. John, *Human Resources Management*, 13th Edition, South Western Cengage Learning, 2011

Merriam Webster, *Websters Ninth New Collegiate Dictionary*, 1988.

Heneman, Herbert, G. III, Heneman, Robert, L. Judge, Timothy, A. *Staffing Organizations*, 2nd Edition, The Mcgraw-Hill Company, Inc. 1997

Internet Sources

https://youtu.be/RyTQ5-SQYTo

http://www.ted.com/talks/lang/en/amy_cuddy_your_body_language_shapes_who_you_are.html

http://www.ted.com/talks/margaret_heffernan_dare_to_disagree.html

http://www.ted.com/talks/lang/en/barry_schwartz_on_our_loss_of_wisdom.html

http://www.ted.com/talks/lang/en/drew_dudley_everyday_leadership.html

http://www.ted.com/talks/simon_sinek_how_great_leaders_inspire_action.html?source=email#.T5Wc3b4ulWh.email

http://www.ted.com/talks/lang/en/shawn_achor_the_happy_secret_to_better_work.html

http://thegroundfloor.typepad.com – Trisha Riggs

https://www2.calstate.edu/csu-system/news/Pages/Move-Over-Millennials-How-iGen-Is-Different-Than-Any-Other-Generation-.aspx

https://www.skillsyouneed.com/ips/conduct-meeting.html

http://checklist.com/meeting-preparation-checklist/ - Collaboration, A Checklist for Planning Your Next Big Meeting, Harvard Business Review,

https://www.forbes.com/sites/work-in-progress/2013/01/15/how-multitasking-hurts-your-brain-and-your-effectiveness-at-work/#3ed4e60c1013

https://www.extension.harvard.edu/professional-development/blog/10-tips-improving-your-public-speaking-skills

https://www.washingtonpost.com/news/wonk/wp/2014/10/30/clowns-are-twice-as-scary-to-democrats-as-they-are-to-republicans/?utm_term=.5d9f0870aad6

https://ideas.ted.com/9-common-sense-rules-for-getting-the-most-out-of-meetings/

https://www.ted.com/talks/mikael_cho_the_science_of_stage_fright_and_how_to_overcome_it

http://sixminutes.dlugan.com/speech-transitions/

http://sixminutes.dlugan.com/pathos-examples-speaking/

https://www.speechanddebate.org/wp-content/uploads/Tips-For-Writing-A-Persuasive-Speech.pdf

https://forbes.com/sites/travisbradberry/2014/10/08/multitasking-damages-your-brain-and-career-new-studies-suggest/#333735e91ee0

https://www.psychologytoday.com/us/blog/the-wide-wide-world-psychology/201704/why-and-how-you-should-take-breaks-work

https://www.coachingpositiveperformance.com/11-symptoms-poor-time-management/

CPSIA information can be obtained
at www.ICGtesting.com
Printed in the USA
BVHW082233290120
570914BV00004B/15/J